WALES: SOUTH AND WEST

JOHN B. HILLING

WALES: SOUTH AND WEST

B. T. Batsford Ltd.,
London & Sydney

First published 1976

© John B. Hilling 1976

Computer typeset by Input Typesetting Ltd, London S.E.1.
and printed in Great Britain by
Biddles Ltd, Guildford, Surrey
for the Publishers B. T. Batsford Ltd
4 Fitzhardinge Street, London W1H 0AH
23 Cross Street, Brookvale, N.S.W. 2100, Australia

ISBN 0 7134 3057 5

CONTENTS

ACKNOWLEDGEMENTS

The publishers and author would like to thank the following for the photographs in this book: Peter Baker nos 1, 19; J. Allan Cash nos 4, 12; Noel Habgood nos 3, 18; A. F. Kersting nos 5, 6, 7, 8, 9, 10, 11, 13, 16; Edwin Smith nos 2, 14, 15, 17; Spectrum no 20.

ILLUSTRATIONS

Cyflwynedig i Shelagh

CHAPTER ONE

Introduction To Southern Wales

Southern Wales comprises Glamorgan *(Sir Forgannwg)*, Gwent *(Sir Fynwy)* or Monmouthshire, as it used to be called, and most of the old county of Breconshire *(Sir Brycheiniog)* which is now part of the new county of Powys. The fact that the region includes Wales' chief industrial areas and contains almost two thirds of the country's population should not deter the traveller for these features are only part of the story. Just as it is wrong to think of Cardiff, the capital, as being nothing more than a scruffy coal port, it is also completely erroneous to imagine the southern part of Wales as being a vast coalfield covered with eyesores. In fact the coalfield and heavily populated districts account for less than half the area. Indeed, some of the most beautiful scenery in Wales is in the south while the omnipresent mountains mean that the countryside is never very far away. Even in the heart of Cardiff the surrounding hills can be seen beyond the buildings and one is aware of a relationship between town and country.

The south divides into four natural regions each with its own characteristics. First, there is the coastal strip which includes the charming Vale of Glamorgan and the Gower peninsula. This is really an undulating plain of limestone and younger rocks which has been uplifted to form a plateau which ends abruptly by the sea in a long line of cliffs. The coastal scenery is most splendid towards the west in the Gower peninsula and much of the peninsula has been designated as an Area of Outstanding Natural Beauty. The three main ports of Wales, Cardiff, Swansea and Newport are situated further east along the coast where the rivers break through

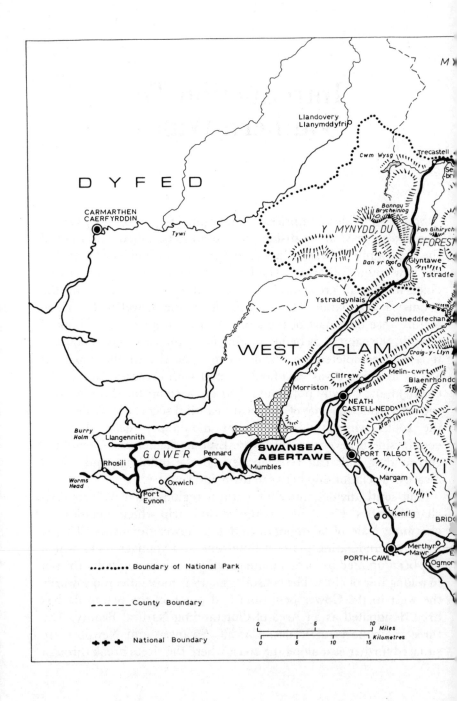

Boundary of National Park

County Boundary

National Boundary

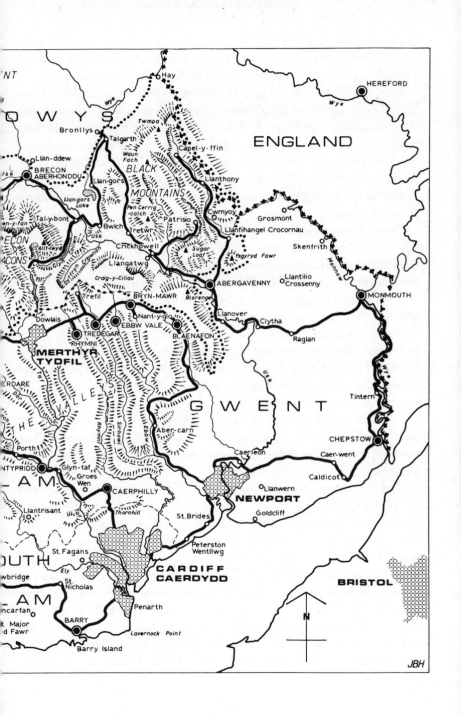

to the sea. Elsewhere along the coastal strip there are low flatlands comprising either large areas of sand dunes or artificially drained agricultural country reminiscent of the East Anglian fens.

Gwent, the second region, is almost an inland extension of the first. This is gently rolling countryside with hills and woods rather than mountains and forests. Most of it is fairly low-lying Old Red Sandstone marls drained towards the west by the lower reaches of the Usk river. To the south-east there is a long limestone ridge through which the Wye river has carved its serpentine course with dramatically scenic results to provide another Area of Outstanding Natural Beauty.

Next, there is the Brecon Beacons National Park, scenically the *pièce de résistance* of southern Wales. Here the richly verdant upper Usk valley stands out in splendid contrast to the wilder uplands on either side. To the east the Black Mountains rise up in a solid block of long parallel ridges ending in a number of isolated mountains around Abergavenny. West of the Usk the Brecon Beacons themselves fan out from a central trio of shapely peaks nearly 3,000 feet high. Beyond are the now empty expanses of the ancient Fforest Fawr (Great Forest) and then Y Mynydd Du and its mysterious lakes. Immediately south of the Beacons and Fforest Fawr a narrow band of limestone, grey-white in colour in contrast to the rich red-browns of the rocks and soils elsewhere, forms the limit of the Park. Here, the action of water on the limestone has resulted in a totally different landscape which includes spectacular waterfalls and caves.

Finally, there are the much-maligned valleys, lying in the kidney-shaped coalfield between the National Park and the Vale of Glamorgan. Certainly, there is industry and ugliness here, but not the appalling mess that one usually associates with large urban areas. Until the coming of industry the long coalfield valleys must have had much the same appearance as the long, narrow valleys of the Black Mountains. Fortunately, the steep sides of the valleys have forced a limit on urban sprawl and today it is still the elongated mountain ridges that dominate the scene and not the buildings and industrial waste. In places the mountain scenery, particularly at the upper end of the Cwm Rhondda, is almost

Alpine in its grandeur but above all it is the unique relationship of towns and countryside that is here so fascinating.

Of the four regions, it was, as might have been expected, the lowland ones – Gwent, the Vale of Glamorgan and Gower – which were always the most attractive to the invader. The Romans set up one of their legionary fortresses at Caerleon, where the Usk valley meets the coastal plain and from there, with the aid of smaller forts placed at regular intervals, they controlled the whole of southern and western Wales. When the Romans arrived they faced a hostile tribe under the command of the heroic figure of Caradog, a refugee prince from south-eastern England. For more than a quarter of a century the Silurians, as this tribe is known to historians, parried the attacks of the Roman garrison based at Gloucester but in the end they were inevitably defeated. The conquerors encouraged the Silurians to move from their hill-fort at Llanmelin and build a new tribal capital on Roman lines at Venta Silurum. Caer-went in Gwent not only retains in its name a memory of this tribal capital but also the well-preserved remains of its defence walls.

In the atmosphere of general unrest that pervaded the whole of the Roman empire at the beginning of the fifth century the imperial army was withdrawn from Britain and the Celts were left to their own defences. The Celts of southern Wales were left to defend the Romano-British heritage for in Wales the Silurians were the people who had been most affected by the Roman occupation and stimulated by their culture. Soon they were to feel the full force of Saxon attacks in the long war of attrition inflicted by the heathen invaders from the east. The southern Celts, however, miraculously succeeded in resisting the Saxons and largely as a result of this Wales became the only part of the western Roman Empire which did not succumb to the pagans.

In the centuries between the departure of the Romans and the arrival of the Normans the three provinces that made up southern Wales – Glywysing, Gwent and Brycheiniog – stayed largely apart from the spasmodic but gradually developing political unity of the rest of Wales. Perhaps it was because so much energy and sacrifice had been expended on defending their homeland that the native princes of the south were so independent.

In other ways the people of the south were not so isolated. They shared in the developing Welsh culture and they still maintained links abroad. Archaeological finds at Dinas Powys hill-fort near Cardiff, for instance, prove that trade was still carried on with Mediterranean lands. The growth of Christianity also meant that there were continuing links with Ireland and France. It seems, indeed, that southern Wales was something of a hot-bed of the Early Christian faith. Llantwit Major and Llancarfan became famous Celtic monasteries and with their missionaries, notably St Patrick, helped to rekindle the flame of Christianity in Ireland. Nothing now remains of the buildings of these and other centres of religion and scholarship but in the coastal strip of Glamorgan alone no less than 26 sculptured Celtic crosses have survived.

Gradually, a unity developed between Glywysing and Gwent which from about the eighth century onwards became known as Morgannwg, after Morgan ap Athrwys and it is from this that the modern name Glamorgan is derived. At its greatest extent Morgannwg stretched from the Tawe to the Wye and included large parts of modern Herefordshire. For a few brief years, in the middle of the eleventh century, Morgannwg and Brycheiniog became politically united with the rest of Wales under Gruffydd ap Llywelyn but then in 1065 Harold conquered a large part of Gwent and annexed it to his earldom of Hereford.

Within two years, following the overthrow of Harold in the epic *coup de grace* at Hastings, the Normans had arrived at the borders of Wales. The first castle to be built by the Normans on the Welsh side of Offa's Dyke was at Chepstow and because of its strategic importance it was constructed in stone. From here, they pushed westwards along the narrow coastal strip towards Dyfed erecting castles as they went, first at Caerleon and then at Cardiff. From Hereford the Norman baron, Bernard de Newmarch set out to conquer Brycheiniog, reaching Brecon by 1093.

The Welsh, refusing to capitulate, withdrew to the hills. By the end of the eleventh century the whole of southern Wales had theoretically fallen to the invader but the conquest was limited in fact to the coastal plains and the Usk and Wye valleys. The hill country of the interior was left in the hands of Welsh rulers subject to the overlordship of the Normans and thus it remained for more than two centuries after the first of the conqueror's incursions. The end of any semblance of Welsh independence in the area came with the building of Caerphilly Castle in 1266 to counter the growing threat of Llywelyn II, the Prince of Wales. Llywelyn destroyed the first castle in 1270 but immediately Gilbert de Clare, the Norman Lord of Glamorgan, started on the construction of a second castle – the greatest fortress in Wales and built in accordance with the most advanced methods of castle building of the day – and Llywelyn was forced to retreat northwards. Twelve years later Llywelyn was ambushed and killed north of Brecon and all Wales fell into English hands.

With the Act of Union between Wales and England in 1536 southern Wales was divided into three counties (Glamorgan, Monmouthshire and Breconshire), organised on the lines of contemporary English shires with county towns at Cardiff, Monmouth and Brecon. During the Civil War, a century later, the whole area was stoutly in support of the King. Raglan Castle, in Gwent, was one of the main Royalist strongholds and became the King's headquarters for a time on his retreat westwards from England. In 1646 Raglan Castle underwent a great siege lasting from June to August; its fall marked the effective end of the first Civil War. Two years later disaffected Parliamentary troops joining with exiled Royalists were routed by Roundheads of the New Model Army in a decisive battle at St Fagans, near Cardiff.

The first appearance of non-conformism in Wales is generally associated with the "gathered church" formed at Llanvaches in Gwent in 1639, although even before this there was reputedly a non-conformist meeting place near Merthyr Tydfil. With the support of the Commonwealth Parliament the Puritan movement grew slowly in the more anglicised areas but with the restoration of the monarchy in 1660 it went into decline. In the early eighteenth century, under the leadership of Howell Harris of Trefecca in Breconshire, non-conformism began to flourish. It was at Caerphilly, in fact, that a historic meeting took place resulting in Welsh Methodists becoming a separate movement adhering to the strict principles of Calvin and thus differing from the Wesleyan

Methodists of England.

Soon the established church was unable to keep pace with the rapid growth of the non-conformists either in influence or in the number of their buildings. Throughout the nineteenth century and the early part of the present century chapel society dominated the religious, cultural and social life of southern Wales. The fecundity of non-conformism resulted in a proliferation of chapels in the Valleys that far outstripped the number of religious buildings found in any other industrial part of Britain. In a society more concerned with rhetoric and revivals than with the visual arts, the chapel was often the only structure in a township which had any architectural pretensions.

During the first half of the eighteenth century, the mountainous hinterland remained virtually unknown and unvisited to outsiders. In 1730, there were only four iron furnaces in what was an almost entirely rural area. Just over a century later there were a hundred and forty furnaces and the industrialisation of the Valleys was well under way. Three quarters of these iron furnaces were situated in a narrow strip at the heads of the valleys between Aberdare and Blaenafon where the necessary ingredients for the industry – iron ore, coal and limestone – were found close together just below the surface. Merthyr Tydfil, with its vast works, soon became the main iron centre of Britain and while men, women and children toiled and sweated and smoke billowed into the sky the finished iron poured down the valleys in canal barges to the fast-growing ports.

By the middle of the century, coal, which had originally only been mined for the iron furnaces, was being produced for sale and that too followed the iron down to the ports. New coal seams were worked, shafts were sunk, towns and villages sprang up, railways were constructed and flocks of people came in from the rest of Wales and the West of England. By the beginning of the present century, the industrialisation and urbanisation of the Valleys was complete.

Work in the ironworks and coalfields was nearly always dangerous and unhealthy, while life in the Valleys must have often been very harsh and crude. Yet despite the often appalling conditions the spirit of the people was never crushed. Richard

Llewelyn's famous novel *How Green Was My Valley*, for all its sentimentality, wonderfully captures the feeling of the Valleys as they once were. Against an intolerable background, the people tried to forget their exacting living conditions by devoting themselves to religion, politics, education, singing and rugby – features for which the Valleys are still renowned. In the western part of Glamorgan, around Swansea, tinplate manufacture and copper smelting took the place of the iron industry and anthracite coal took the place of steam coal. And just as Cardiff was to become the world's most important coal port, so Swansea became the world's leading metallurgical centre.

But for both Swansea and Cardiff industry is only one side of the coin. Swansea is also no mean seaside resort. Indeed, the view of Swansea Bay fringed by fine sandy beaches overlooked by a modern university has been compared to that of Naples. Cardiff has preserved, almost miraculously, an extraordinarily splendid castle and a magnificent park right at its heart while alongside there is a fine civic centre, which makes it a worthy capital of Wales.

CHAPTER TWO

Cardiff

The visitor approaching Cardiff by road from the east or arriving by train may be excused for thinking that there is nothing distinctly Welsh about the capital city apart from the words *Dinas Caerdydd* (meaning City of Cardiff) that he sees everywhere painted in bold letters on one side of the city's orange buses. On the basis of first impressions one may indeed wonder why Cardiff was chosen to be the capital of Wales for its appearance in the annals of Welsh political history has been almost nil. Like Helsinki, Cardiff today is almost entirely the product of the last century-and-a-half and in a similar way was given its comparatively recent national status by external edict. Yet indisputably, Cardiff is the capital of Wales not only by virtue of its size but because of its importance as the administrative centre and because of its fine historic and nationally important buildings. Moreover, just as the Finnish capital is a bilingual city so is the Welsh capital and though Welsh is in terms of numbers a minority language it is, perhaps surprisingly, spoken by more people in Cardiff than almost any other town in Wales.

The most interesting way of approaching Cardiff is from the valleys to the north and north-west, either over Caerphilly Mountain or through the Taff Gorge or via Llandaf. Whichever way one chooses the immediate impression is of a place which is strikingly different from all other cities. On the two-mile journey from historic Llandaf one is aware, almost all the way, of the great park that follows the Taf river from the outer suburbs to the fantastic pile of Cardiff Castle and links the surrounding countryside with the heart of the city centre. On the northern approaches one passes alongside Cathays Park – a civic centre

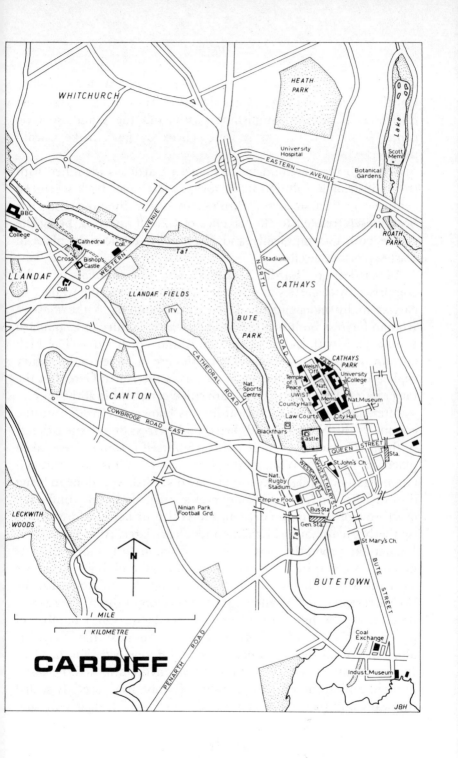

CARDIFF

which is the cultural and administrative heart of Wales as well as Cardiff – before arriving at Cardiff Castle. These three things – the enormous park, the astonishing castle and the grandiose civic centre – all standing, as it were, cheek by jowl, make Cardiff unique.

Although the development of modern Cardiff is identified with the Industrial Revolution its history, in fact, goes back seventeen centuries to Roman times. Throughout all this time the castle has been closely related to the fortunes of Cardiff and this, being the centre both geographically and historically, is the right place to start exploring the city.

As castles go, Cardiff Castle is very unusual for it really comprises three castles in one, each forming part of the whole, yet each visually independent. The earliest building is the massive Roman fortress built at the end of the third century to a standard square plan with gates on the south and north sides. The high curtain walls surrounding the castle are a nineteenth-century replica of the Roman fortress walls, as is the North Gate, but the lower parts of the original walls are still clearly visible at the base.

After the Roman withdrawal little is known of Cardiff until the coming of the Normans and the second fortress on the site belongs to them. The actual founding of Cardiff itself is said to have taken place in 1081 by William the Conqueror on his way through Glamorgan on a pilgrimage to St David's. Little was done to bring the district under the Conqueror's rule, however, until the overthrow of Iestyn ap Gwrgan, the Welsh prince of Morgannwg, by the Norman baron Fitzhamon ten years later. After his success Fitzhamon promptly took over the Roman fort and within its derelict walls raised an enormous mound and built a timber stockade on top of it. All was not well, though, for the Normans. The Welsh resented the invaders and at every opportunity they swept down from the hills to raid and harass them. On a number of occasions they made vigorous attempts to oust the Normans altogether from their conquered lands. On one occasion, in 1158, Ifor ap Meurig, the Welsh lord of Senghenydd, attacked the castle at night and in the words of Giraldus Cambrensis "secretly scaled the walls and seizing the count and countess with their only son, carried them off into the woods and did not release them until he had recovered everything that had been unjustly taken from him." A short time later, the Normans rebuilt the keep in stone and this splendid twelve-sided building – a perfect example of its type – still stands perched high up on the steep mound surrounded by a wide circular moat. In the thirteenth century Gilbert de Clare added a new gatehouse to the keep and built the Black Tower on the site of the Roman south gate. Some time later the town was enclosed in stone walls but these were not sufficient to deter Owain Glyndŵr who broke through the West Gate in 1404, burnt many of the houses and captured the castle.

The third castle, dating mainly from the eighteenth and nineteenth centuries, is really a luxurious castellated mansion built in the south-west corner of the Roman fort. The core of it, comprising the medieval Great Hall and the Octagon Tower, was erected in the mid-fifteenth century following a return to peaceful times after the failure of Glyndŵr's bid for independence. In 1777 it was improved and modernised by Henry Holland. At the same time Holland's famous landscape-gardener father-in-law, 'Capability' Brown, laid out the magnificent Bute Park between the castle and the river. The biggest and most adventurous alterations, however, belong to the late nineteenth century when the third Marquis of Bute decided to employ William Burges to restore the west wing of the castle. Burges was an architect of extraordinary imagination and wit and both these aspects were given free play in his restoration. Burges added towers, rebuilt the Great Hall and completely transformed all the interiors in a most exotic way. For instance, there is the Arab Room, reputedly copied from an Arabian harem, the Chaucer Room with decoration to illustrate his writings, the Guest Room with walls inlaid with minerals and precious stones and the Summer Smoking Room with its domed ceiling lined with mirrors. The result of all these Gothic additions and alterations is an amazing virtuoso piece which has been rightly called "one of the triumphs of nineteenth-century Romantic architecture."

By the nineteenth century the Bute family had taken the place of the former Norman lords in the life and affairs of the city. They owned much of Cardiff and large parts of the valleys as well. They were immensely rich, owning castles in Scotland and Spain, as well as in Wales, but were, fortunately, keenly interested in the development of the town. By the end of the nineteenth century the physical shape and appearance of Cardiff as it then was, and still is to a large extent, was mainly due to the work and influence of the Butes. It was they who built the docks which were to make Cardiff the greatest coal port in the world and it was they who preserved intact the open land north of the castle to provide the city with its magnificent park and space for the civic centre.

The splendid civic centre in Cathays Park just north of the castle is, in fact, the most outstanding architectural phenomenon of twentieth-century Cardiff. It was begun more than seventy years ago and has been gradually developed until now it is almost complete. The heart of the civic centre is a delightful park, known as Alexandra Gardens, around which a dozen or so public buildings are grouped. Appropriately, the Welsh National War Memorial – an elegant temple-like building with a circular colonnade of Corinthian columns – stands in the place of honour at the centre of the gardens surrounded by colourful plants and flowering cherry trees.

The three principal buildings of the civic centre form a line across the southern end of the central park. In the middle is the City Hall, built in 1904, with its superbly designed and brilliantly sculptured clock tower and a domed council chamber surmounted by a snarling dragon. A comparatively austere entrance hall on the ground floor leads via baroque staircases to the Marble Hall and Assembly Hall on the first floor. The Marble Hall is lined on either side with paired marble columns with, in between, statues depicting Celtic and Welsh heroes including Dewi Sant (St David), Hywel Dda, Llywelyn II, Owain Glyndŵr, Henry VII and Boadicea. The Assembly Hall with its richly decorated semi-circular ceiling and elaborate bronze chandeliers is even more splendid. To the left of the City Hall are the Law Courts, designed in a similar but more subdued style.

The National Museum of Wales, to the right of the City Hall, was opened as long ago as 1927 but the building is still incomplete.

Its primary purpose is 'to teach the world about Wales and the Welsh people about their own fatherland' and this it does admirably through its different departments. The monumental main hall of the Museum, with its marble columns and floors glowing in the pink light from the dome above, is an architectural masterpiece. On either side of this are the various exhibition galleries. Those on the lower floors are devoted to botany, zoology, geology, and industry and of these, the latter deserves special mention for its unique and imaginative mock-up of a coalmine. The upper-floor galleries illustrate art and archaeology. Welsh artists, including Richard Wilson, Augustus John, Frank Brangwyn and Ceri Richards, naturally feature prominently in the painting section but there is also an exceptionally fine collection of French Impressionist and Post-Impressionist paintings. The archaeological exhibits cover all the periods from man's first appearance in Wales up to the Middle Ages. The collection of standing stones and Early Christian crosses from the Celtic era is particularly good.

In the Gorsedd Gardens in front of the National Museum there is a circle of standing stones that at first glance looks like a Stone-Age stone circle. It is, in fact, a modern Gorsedd Circle erected for the proclamation ceremony of the National Eisteddfod of Wales when it was held in Cardiff. There are many of these modern stone circles in towns throughout Wales for no National Eisteddfod may be held without a ceremonial proclamation by the Gorsedd of Bards at least a year and a day in advance and each proclamation takes place at a specially built Gorsedd Circle in the place where the festival is to be held. When not in use the regalia for this colourful and picturesque ceremony is displayed in the National Museum. Next to the Gorsedd Circle is a modern bronze statue of the First World War Prime Minister, Earl Lloyd George with outstretched arm and clenched fist, while nearby there is a fine equestrian statue of Lord Tredegar, the captain of the 17th Lancers in the famous 'Charge of the Light Brigade' at Balaclava in 1854.

The most architecturally rewarding building in the civic centre is perhaps the old Glamorgan County Hall, built in 1912 in King Edward VII Avenue. Its graceful and scholarly main front with paired Corinthian columns and beautifully carved sculpture ranks with the best Classical Revival buildings elsewhere. Completely different in architectural treatment is the Temple of Peace and Health further along the road. It was built as a streamlined classical monument to the visionary illusion of the League of Nations and to the ideals of Richard Henry of Tregaron, the Welsh 'Apostle of Peace', and was ironically opened in 1938 on the eve of the Second World War. Other buildings in Cathays Park include the Welsh Office, the University College of South Wales and the University of Wales Institute of Science and Technology.

East of Cardiff Castle is Queen Street and immediately south of the castle and at right angles to Queen Street are High Street and St. Mary Street. These thoroughfares form the shopping and commercial centre of the city and a special feature is the wonderful series of shopping arcades that branch off on both sides of High Street and St Mary Street, to connect with the streets behind.

The only medieval church in the city centre now is St John the Baptist, standing on an island right in the middle of the shopping centre. Its glory is the graceful Perpendicular-style tower topped by an exquisitely detailed parapet and delicate lantern pinnacles. The tower was built in 1453 by John Hart, the master mason who was also responsible for the similar and more famous tower at Wrexham in northern Wales. In the Middle Ages there were three other churches in Cardiff. St Mary's, the parish church, stood at the southern end of St Mary Street, but it was too close to the banks of the Afon Taf and was washed away by the river in the seventeenth century. The other two churches formed part of friaries sited on either side of Cardiff Castle. The Franciscan friary has now gone (although the name is still perpetuated in Greyfriars Road) but the foundations of the Dominican, or Black Friars', friary can still be seen in Bute Park alongside the castle.

The Taf continued to cause trouble until the mid-nineteenth century when it was then diverted on a more westerly course in order that land could be reclaimed to build the General Railway Station. Westgate Street follows approximately the old course of the river and a side street nearby called Quay Street is a reminder of the days when large boats could come up river almost as far as the castle.

Much of the reclaimed land immediately west of Westgate Street is devoted to sport. Here is the famous Cardiff Arms Park with its two rugby football stadia – one for Welsh internationals and the other for the Cardiff Rugby Club. When an international is being played the adjoining streets resound to the echoing roars of the crowd and the swelling chords of "Calon Lan", sung as only Welsh rugby supporters can sing it. Nearby is the Empire Pool, built in 1958 when the Empire Games were held in Cardiff.

Just beyond the bridge across the river, in Cowbridge Road, is the terrace house where the composer Ivor Novello was born in 1893. His first song was published when he was only 15 and he later became an actor manager. He is remembered most of all, however, for songs such as 'Keep the home fires burning' and 'We'll gather lilacs'. Howard Spring, the author of *Fame is the Spur* was another Cardiffian born not far away at Canton in 1889.

For the capital of Wales Cardiff has a curiously cosmopolitan population. This is most evident in the multi-racial community of Butetown immediately south of the city centre where one can see an Islamic mosque, a Byzantine temple and a Scandinavian church. As the docks area Butetown attracted people from all over the world and was for long known disparagingly as 'Tiger Bay'.

Butetown starts at the old Custom House, built appropriately alongside the Glamorganshire Canal, at the southern end of St Mary Street. The historic canal has now been filled in but its site can still be made out in a number of places. It was the opening of the canal in 1794 which more than anything else led to the subsequent development of Cardiff as a major port, for without the canal there would have been no outlet for the export of iron and coal from the Valleys. Construction of the canal was followed by the building of the docks by the Bute family in 1839, 1859, 1874 and 1907. Rapid expansion of trade followed the opening of each dock and this in turn was followed by a dramatic increase in population which rose from less than two thousand in 1801 to more than 160,000 a century later.

During the first half of the nineteenth century most of Cardiff's building expansion took place in Butetown in the narrow wedge of land between the docks and the canal. Bute Street developed as a fashionable area and later the southern end of Butetown, near the Pierhead, became the main business centre of Cardiff. Most of Butetown has been rebuilt over the years but some of its best buildings still remain. St Mary's Church, a nineteenth-century successor to the medieval building and an early example of the Romanesque Revival, stands at the town end of Bute Street. At the seaward end the boldly pompous Coal Exchange in Mount Stuart Square has been restored and is worth a visit. Inside it has a vast hall, elaborately panelled in wood, with tiers of encircling balconies supported on timber columns. Even more exotic from the outside is the brick-red Pierhead Building erected in 1896 as the headquarters of the Bute Docks Company. It stands in proud isolation on the edge of the harbour and at the entrance to the docks as an imposing French Gothic landmark with pinnacled turrets and a castellated clock tower. Nearby an impressive Industrial and Maritime Museum is being developed.

In complete contrast to the busy commerce and industry of Butetown is the village city of Llandaf on the northern side of the city centre. Today Llandaf forms part of Cardiff but for centuries it maintained a separate and independent existence both as a lordship and as a borough with its own market and fair. Although only two miles from the centre of the capital, it still retains its own distinctive identity partly as a result of its geographical isolation from the rest of Cardiff and partly due to the architectural character and quality of its buildings. Its separateness is best appreciated when approached on foot through the great expanse of parkland that stretches northwards alongside the river from Cardiff Castle to Llandaf Fields. From here, the spire of Llandaf Cathedral can be seen through the trees in an almost rural setting.

Although fairly small when compared to the greater English cathedrals, Llandaf Cathedral is full of interest and what it lacks in size it more than makes up for in antiquity. Indeed, this is one of the oldest church sites in Britain with a history going back to the Early Christian saints of the sixth century – well before the time when St Augustine came to establish Christianity in southern England. The earliest monastery, probably built in timber, has disappeared without trace and likewise the first small stone church although a tenth-century Celtic cross in the south presbytery aisle is a reminder of this period. Since these rudimentary beginnings the cathedral has been rebuilt or restored five times. The earliest parts still existing are the early twelfth-century Romanesque arches in the presbytery and the aisles. From about 1170 onwards the church was largely rebuilt when the nave was extended westwards in early Gothic style. The fine Perpendicular-style Jasper tower complete with elaborately decorated pinnacles was added at the west end in the late fifteenth century.

By the eighteenth century the cathedral had become derelict and a classical temple, designed by John Wood of Bath, was erected within the ruins. In the nineteenth century the temple was demolished and the cathedral largely rebuilt by John Prichard, a distinguished local architect. He was responsible for completing the west front and adding the splendid tower and spire (195 feet high) which gives the cathedral a dignity and importance which it never had before. Through the influence of Prichard's partner, John Seddon, many fine Pre-Raphaelite works of art were added to the interior. Notable amongst them is Rossetti's triptych *The Seed of David* in St Illtud's Chapel.

Inside the cathedral the most impressive part of the medieval building is the superbly decorated Romanesque chancel arch through which can be seen the delicate roof vaulting of the thirteenth-century Lady Chapel. Equally striking is the modern parabolic concrete arch at the junction of the nave and choir. It supports a cylindrical organ case decorated with a large aluminium sculpture of Christ in Majesty and was added when the cathedral was restored once again in the 1960's after being bombed and burnt out during the Second World War.

On the hill above the cathedral is the Green, an informal open space surrounded by varied buildings that gives Llandaf much of its 'village' character. The City Cross, traditionally the place where Archbishop Baldwin (accompanied by Giraldus Cambrensis) preached the Third Crusade in 1188, stands in the centre of the Green. Behind this are the craggy remains of the old Cathedral Bell-tower built in the thirteenth century as a detached campanile.

The massive twin-towered gatehouse at the end of the Green forms the entrance to the Bishop's Castle, now a picturesque shell with a large courtyard enclosed by high curtain walls and corner towers. Although for long associated with the Bishops of Llandaf it is more likely to have been built by the Norman Lord of Glamorgan at the end of the thirteenth century. The ruined upper parts of the towers are a reminder of Owain Glyndŵr's vendetta against the Normans' descendants. The castle now forms the garden entrance to the Cathedral School at the rear. This three-storey Georgian house, at one time the Bishop's Palace, was probably designed by John Wood at the time he built the temple in the ruins of the cathedral.

The greatest attraction of Cardiff is, perhaps even more than its historic castles and fine public buildings, the outstanding series of parks in and around the city. The fact that they are often associated with other interesting places only enhances their attraction. The most popular is Roath Park, a long, narrow open space with playing fields at one end, botanical gardens in the centre and a large boating lake at the other end. The lighthouse in the lake is the Scott Memorial built to commemorate the occasion when Captain Scott sailed from Cardiff in the *Terra Nova* in 1910 on his last heroic journey to Antarctica.

The stream that feeds the lake at Roath Park comes down from Parc Cefn On nestling amongst the chain of hills on the northern outskirts of the city. In springtime the dingle in Parc Cefn On is a riot of colour from the rhododendrons and azaleas but much of this upland park is either forest or open moorland with panoramic views of Cardiff and the Severn Sea. Another forest-park with excellent views is the Wenallt north of Rhiwbina. This is on an outlying spur of the main line of hills and as such was an obvious site for a hill-fort in the Dark Ages. It is just possible to make out the ramparts of the hill-fort even now. Just below the Wenallt a small castle motte survives from the twelfth century. This is known as the Twmpath and is traditionally supposed to have been the scene of a fierce battle between Iestyn ap Gwrgan, the last native prince of Morgannwg (Glamorgan), and the Normans. So much blood was shed at the battle that a nearby stream is still called

Nant Waedlyd, or the 'Bloody Brook'.

On the crest of the ridge at Thornhill the remains of Castell Morgraig lie hidden and half buried amongst the trees. This was a castle built by the Welsh princes in the early thirteenth century, but it was overwhelmed by the invaders before being fully completed.

Further west the Normans built Castell Coch in a fairy-tale setting at the entrance to the Taff Gorge to guard the route against attacks by the Welsh from the north. Perched upon the side of the steep hill against a backcloth of trees it has an unusual triangular layout with three circular towers capped by conical roofs and is reminiscent of a Rhineland castle. This is partly the result of restoration in the late nineteenth century by William Burges and Lord Bute. Basically, however, the castle that can be seen today is, from the outside at least, the same as the one built by Gilbert de Clare at the end of the thirteenth century. The inside, on the other hand, is totally different for here Burges indulged in a sumptous extravaganza of Victorian decoration and invention only equalled by his interiors at Cardiff Castle. The octagonal Drawing Room with its encircling gallery, profuse decoration and wonderful rib-vaulted ceiling is a brilliantly conceived space. The cellar dungeon is a complete contrast with bare stone walls and no light save from two tiny holes precisely positioned so that both streams of daylight meet in a small square patch in the centre of the floor.

Castell Coch itself is in another forest-park and after looking at the castle one can go for long walks on the hills or through the woods. Yet another park with a castle is at St Fagans, an attractive village on the western side of the city. It is a park with a difference, however, for this is the Welsh Folk Museum – a 'must' for anyone interested in the social history and the traditional life and culture of Wales. The museum was established in the grounds of St Fagan's Castle in 1946 through the benevolence of Lord Plymouth and is similar to the open-air museums in Scandinavia.

The hundred-acre museum is in two parts. The first part is a modern museum with excellent exhibition galleries built around an open courtyard. From the open colonnaded exhibition area near the lower entrance the visitor can walk through the various galleries in an ascending spiral to the restaurant on the upper floor. The second part is the folk-park which surrounds the exhibition building and where the physical background to Welsh rural life has been lovingly and painstakingly re-created with buildings. Here one can see carefully rebuilt cottages and farmhouses from all parts of Wales, a woollen factory that still makes and sells textiles, a leather tannery, a smithy from Powys, a three-storey cornmill, a tollgate house and an early non-conformist chapel from Dyfed, and an eighteenth-century cockpit that once stood in the yard of an inn in Clwyd.

An important part of the museum is St Fagan's Castle itself. This is a typical Elizabethan mansion, whitewashed and with many high gables. The rooms on the two lower floors are open to the public and have been richly furnished according to the period with furniture collected from houses in different parts of Wales. Amongst the furnishings are fine panelled ceilings and walls, elaborately carved fireplaces, tapestries, paintings and harps. The grounds immediately outside the mansion have been beautifully laid out with formal gardens and beyond there are terraces stepping down towards a delightful little valley filled by a chain of small fishponds.

Finally there is Penarth on the headland immediately south of Cardiff. The Ely river separates the two towns and has helped to preserve the separate identity of Penarth, although otherwise it is now almost a part of the capital. In the mid-nineteenth century, however, it was merely an isolated and straggling village with a tiny gable-towered church overlooking the sea. The church was, in spite of its diminutive size, a landmark for sailors and when the town developed into a port and a new St Augustine's Church was built in 1866, William Butterfield, the architect, decided to keep to the same type of gable tower in order to conform to the Admiralty charts. The exterior has a striking simplicity but it is the interior that really compels attention. The walls between the yellow and pink columns and arches are filled with geometric patterns of multi-coloured brickwork giving the inside a feeling of warmth and light that it is without equal in any other church built in Wales during the nineteenth century.

Although Penarth was developed as a port it also became a favourite residence for the shipping and coal owners. Indeed, at one time there were reputed to be ten millionaires living in the town. They turned their backs on the dock area north of the headland and developed instead the southern part of the town with a pier, a long esplanade and colourful gardens. The dock has closed but the pier still survives and behind it a delightful dingle winds up through Alexandra Park to the town centre. Near the upper entrance of the park is Turner House, a building erected in 1888 by James Pyke Thompson as a private art gallery and now forming a branch of the National Museum. It was named in memory of the painter J. M. W. Turner and now houses paintings, period furniture and *objets d'art* as well as numerous temporary exhibitions, all in an atmosphere of elegant informality.

South of Penarth pier there is a fine cliff walk to Lavernock Point. It was between Lavernock Point and the island of Flatholm that Guglielmo Marconi transmitted the first radio message across water on 11 May 1897. The historic message was brief and to the point and simply said: 'Are you ready?' A plaque outside Lavernock church records the event and a copy of the message is kept in the National Museum in Cardiff.

CHAPTER THREE

The Valleys

If Cardiff has not in the past been generally regarded as a city of distinction, in spite of its architectural treasures, the mining Valleys to the north have been even less well-treated. A. E. Trueman's comment in his *Geology and Scenery of England and Wales* on 'the excessive ugliness of these industrial towns' is fairly typical but misses the point. In comparison with most other large industrial areas of Britain the Valleys are scenically attractive and this is simply because they are valleys; the landscape dominates the townscape and the steepness of the intervening mountains has by and large prevented urban sprawl. The Valleys and their surroundings are full of interest and no one can claim to know southern Wales unless they have seen them at first hand.

Like Cardiff, the Valleys as we know them today are very much the products of the Industrial Revolution. They are the consequences of the tremendous changes that took place from the middle of the eighteenth century onwards when, first the wealth of iron, and then the riches of coal were systematically exploited. During the first half of the eighteenth century, the Valleys remained unknown and unvisited, a semi-wild area of thickly wooded valleys and barren hills, isolated farmsteads and here and there a few small villages. Roads were virtually non-existent and the few that did exist were usually unmade and unfenced tracks along the mountain ridges. There were only three places of any consequence – Caerphilly, Merthyr Tydfil and Llantrisant – and even these were little more than glorified villages.

In the two centuries that have passed since then much has changed. Indeed, in some ways the wheel has turned full circle –

the ironworks have come and gone, their scarred landscapes gradually being reclaimed, and collieries are no longer such familiar sights as they once were. Yet much remains, both of the often dramatic and sometimes exquisite natural scenery and of the far-reaching ingenuity of man, to make a tour of the Valleys a fascinating experience.

The road from Cardiff sweeps up and across Caerphilly Common and then down at a steep angle into Caerphilly itself. From the top of the ridge Caerphilly can be seen spread out in a rather formless pattern, unusual for a valley town, with Caerphilly Castle right in the middle. This view immediately gives the lie to the idea that the Valleys are in any way uninteresting for here, well within the southern belt of the coalfield and yet only seven miles from Cardiff, is one of the most outstanding castles in Europe. It is, in fact, the largest and most formidable fortress in Wales covering an area of thirty acres and comprising a concentric citadel surrounded by an inner moat which in turn is defended by two artificial lakes (incorporating a fortified man-made island), a tremendous stone barrage wall to hold back the water and an outer moat. The castle was started in 1271 and was built, not by a king as its scale would suggest, but by Gilbert de Clare, a Norman baron, as a redoubt to withstand the threats of Llywelyn ap Gruffydd, Prince of Wales. No other castle in Britain has such a complex system of defence and counter-defence.

Like the great Edwardian castles in the north Caerphilly Castle is not only a monument to the genius and power of the invaders but also, and perhaps even more so, a tribute to the ferocious persistence of the Welsh princes and the sacrificial bravery of their followers, for this is what made such a colossal fortress necessary. Once the castle had been completed the multiple defence system made it virtually impregnable: it was almost useless to attempt to capture it. By that time Edward I had conquered Wales and without the leadership of their own princes, the Welsh settled for an uneasy peace. Nevertheless, by 1316 war had broken out again and in that year Llywelyn Bren of Senghenydd besieged the castle for more than a month until, with the help of troops from Pembroke, Gloucester, Somerset and Dorset, he was outflanked by the

Anglo-Normans and forced to withdraw to the mountains. Lady de Clare, who had the misfortune to be at Caerphilly at the time, was hurriedly rescued and taken back to the safety of Cardiff Castle. For nearly a century there was peace again until Prince Owain Glyndŵr besieged the castle and captured it for a short period.

Thereafter, the castle was not involved in any further wars. Even the celebrated "leaning tower of Caerphilly" was not the direct result of war damage but the consequence of a deliberate policy of demolition in the seventeenth century by Royalist forces to prevent the castle being used by the Parliamentary army during the Civil War. After that the castle gradually deteriorated. Now, as a result of restorations carried out by the Marquis of Bute and the Department of the Environment it is possible to see how majestic and stupendous a fortress this must have appeared in the Middle Ages.

For most people living outside the area the name Caerphilly means only one thing – cheese, or *Caws Caerffili* as it used to be known locally. The origin of Caerphilly cheese, a creamy cheese which matures quickly and is best eaten when fresh, is obscure for it is only comparatively recently that it has gained fame. Cheese was certainly produced in the farms of Gwent and Glamorgan for centuries and presumably it got its popular name because most of it was brought to the Cheese Market at Caerphilly for sale. It was not until the end of the nineteenth century that its fame grew; by then two and half tons a week were sold in the market. It has always been especially popular with colliers, who found that it was an ideal food to sustain them during the long hours underground. During the Second World War the Government banned its manufacture. Afterwards there was very little interest in it locally and for years Caerphilly cheese seems to have been made everywhere, even in Holland and New Zealand, except in Wales. Now once again it is made in its home-town.

Two of the chapels near Caerphilly are important in the history of Welsh non-conformism. Groes Wen, a couple of miles west of the town, was the first Methodist chapel in Wales when it was built in 1742. Just to the south is Watford, which was built four years earlier as an Independent chapel. It was here that the first synod of the newly created Welsh Calvinistic Methodist Church, now known as the Presbyterian Church of Wales, was held in 1743. A man who was connected with both chapels from the beginning was William Edwards, the famous bridge builder. He was appointed pastor of Capel Groes Wen in 1745 and continued in that capacity until his death in 1789. Edwards was a man of many parts. Before his appointment he was already well known locally as a stonemason, building houses and barns in the district as well as a mill, and at the early age of 21 was responsible for erecting an iron forge for a Cardiff ironworks.

William Edwards' most spectacular feat was the design and construction in 1756 of an elegant new bridge across the Taf at Pontypridd, a few miles away to the west. Later Edwards and his sons were to build numerous handsome bridges throughout southern Wales, but none were so graceful and daring, or as large as this functional masterpiece. Indeed, at the time of its erection, it was probably the largest single-arch bridge in Europe, with a clear span of 140 feet, a size not surpassed until the new London Bridge was built in 1921! Success was not easily achieved and Edwards' first attempts to span the Taf, in 1746 and 1751, ended in failure. Nothing daunted, the self-made mason decided to overcome the problem of the bridge's self-weight by piercing the spandrels with cylindrical holes, three on each side reducing in size as they ascend the arch and providing at one and the same time a reduction in weight, channels for the passage of floodwaters and a restrained decorative pattern. In 1857 a crude three-arch bridge was built alongside, rudely conflicting in appearance with Edwards' rainbow-like stone bridge. The original bridge still survives, however, and is now used for pedestrians only.

In the nineteenth century Pontypridd was the home of Evan James and his son James James, who between them wrote and composed the Welsh national anthem *Hen Wlad fy Nhadau*. Evan James was a weaver who had moved from Argoed in the Sirhowi valley to Pontypridd after buying a woollen mill there. In his spare time he was a poet and it was he who wrote the words of the anthem, while his son composed the melody. It was published four years later in 1860, and then became immediately popular and was sung at numerous *eisteddfodau* until it became accepted as the national anthem. A fine memorial by Sir Goscombe John of the father and son stands in Ynyshangarad Park near to William Edwards' old bridge.

A memorial of a different kind overlooks the new dual carriageway road at Glyn-taf just south of Pontypridd. This is a pair of unusual three-storey, circular stone houses erected about 1838 by the eccentric Dr William Price. They were the entrance lodges for an eight-storey-high druidic palace and museum, intended to be erected at the pseudo-druidical site of Y Maen Chwyf (The Rocking Stone) nearby. In the event the Round Houses, or Druid Towers as they are otherwise known, were the only part of the plan carried out, for Price failed to get any support for his appeal for subscriptions and in any case he did not even own the land on which the houses were built!

Although fully qualified and well respected as a physician and surgeon, Dr. Price's unconventional ways and heretical ideas must have seemed very strange to the people around him. For one thing he claimed to be an arch-druid and made a practice of performing ancient rites on the Rocking Stone at Pontypridd. Then there was the way he dressed and lived. *The Dictionary of Welsh Biography* puts it well and succinctly: 'His dress consisted of a white tunic, covering a scarlet waistcoat, while his trousers were of green cloth. On his head he wore a huge fox skin. He practised free-love, advocated cremation, was a vegetarian, scorned religion, despised the law and its administration, and was a Chartist leader. After the Chartist march on Newport in 1839, he escaped to France disguised as a woman.' Dr Price will be remembered more than anything, however, for his advocacy of cremation. Matters were brought to a head in 1884 when his five-month-old son died. Dr Price was then 84 years old and his son, named Iesu Grist (Jesus Christ) was the offspring of his young companion, Gwenllian Llewelyn. Price took the body of the baby to Caerlan Hill near Llantrisant and there attempted to cremate it. Soon afterwards the police arrived and snatched the partly consumed body from the coffin while the watching crowd, now frantic with rage, tried to throw the doctor into the fire. Price was brought to trial in Cardiff but was not convicted and as a result the legality of cremation was established. In 1893 Dr Price died at Llantrisant and in accordance with the explicit and detailed instructions contained in his will, he was cremated in front of thousands of onlookers, the first of innumerable official cremations.

Pontypridd is sited at the junction of the Taf and Rhondda rivers and because of its position naturally became the focus of all the coal traffic coming down to Cardiff from the two Rhondda valleys and from the Taf and Dar valleys. The railway station there, with its elegant curving canopies, has the longest platforms in Wales and in its heyday was one of the busiest, if not the busiest, junction in the principality; in those days, as many as 250 trains of all descriptions passed through Pontypridd every 24 hours.

There are two Rhondda valleys – the Rhondda Fawr (Great) and Rhondda Fach (Little) – which join together at Porth a few miles north-west of Pontypridd. Apart from some isolated farmsteads there had been no real settlement of these valleys prior to the expansion of coal mining. Indeed, before the industrialisation of the Valleys, the Rhondda was a sublimely picturesque place. Thomas Roscoe described it in 1836 as 'wild and mountainous where nature seemed to reign in stern and unbroken silence amidst her own eternal rocks. Not a human being beside myself appeared to be breaking these solitudes nor was a habitation to be seen.' The opening of coalmines brought about great changes to the area, but was not so catastrophic as one might expect; even in the heart of the Rhondda the open countryside, in the form of craggy cliffs, mountainous moorlands and coniferous forests, is never far away.

Before 1860 development had only just started at the lower end of the main valley, but by the end of the nineteenth century, both valleys were completely built-up. Within 40 years the population had soared dramatically from 4,000 to about 115,000 and continued to rise until the depression of the 1930's caused it to decline. In the deeply etched valleys land was at a premium due to the very small proportion of it that was suitable for residential development, either because the remainder was too steep, or was too valuable for coal working. Housing in the form of terraces clinging to the valley sides, parallel to the river, road and railway,

41

was the most economical way of using the precious land and it, therefore, became the predominant type of development. The earliest housing was often in isolated, single-storey rows with gardens at the back and front, but in the later two-storey terraces built in blocks around the pitheads the front gardens were omitted. All the available space between each pithead settlement was then filled with more terraces so that eventually there was a continuous chain of urban development, punctuated by nearly 50 collieries and more than 150 chapels, extending from the confluence of the two rivers at Porth right back to the blind ends of the valleys.

Now there are only three collieries working in the Rhondda. Many of the chapels have been demolished or closed. On the whole, though, despite the large number of chapels, the Rhondda does not have any really good-looking examples. The best are Capel Siloh at Pentre and Capel Salem at Porth and both date from the 1870's. Another chapel of interest, though unexceptional to look at, is Capel Jerusalem at Ton Pentre. This is one of the largest in the valley and was sometimes called the 'Methodist Cathedral of the Rhondda'. Its minister and designer was the Rev William Jones who had trained as a carpenter before going into the ministry. After coming to Capel Jerusalem at the age of 29 he renewed his first interest and as well as rebuilding his own chapel, he designed more than 200 chapels elsewhere in Wales.

One of the Rhondda's most celebrated sons was Griffith Morgan, a fabulous cross-country runner born at the beginning of the eighteenth century at Llanwynno. He is better known as Guto Nyth-brân after the name of the farm where he lived. Many of the stories about him are probably fiction, but one at least seems to be true. According to this tale his sudden death at the age of 37 was the result of running the twelve miles from Newport to Bedwas Church in the incredible time of 53 minutes. A cross-country race through the streets of the neighbouring valleys is held every New Year's Eve in Guto's honour.

Blaenrhondda at the head of Rhondda Fawr lies in the valley bottom in the midst of some of the most dramatic and magnificent mountain scenery in the southern part of Wales. The valley sides here rise steeply for almost 1,000 feet up to bands of great cliffs before flattening out into the softer moorlands of the mountain ridges. Until the 1930's there was no exit from the valley at this end and, in fact, both valleys were, for all practical purposes, completely hemmed-in and isolated except for a couple of outlets at the southern end. It's an ill wind, however, that blows no good and during the long years of the depression unemployed miners built a new road out of the northern end of the main valley and across the moorland ridge to connect with the other valleys and provide an alternative outlet for the Rhondda. At its highest point of 1,625 feet the road is not far from the summit of Craig y Llyn and then suddenly it descends in a series of dramatic hairpin bends across the northern escarpment of the mountain and down to the col that separates the Nedd and Dâr valleys. From the road there are fine views of the Fforest Fawr and the Brecon Beacons to the north. Though tempting, these mountains are best approached from the Usk valley further north.

After the narrowness of the Rhondda valleys the openness of the country around Aberdare is an unexpected contrast. The mountains are very much in evidence but they are gentler, and Aberdare itself lies in a bowl giving it the appearance of a market town rather than an industrial conglomeration. The illusion is helped by the fact that St John's Church in its tree-lined churchyard is still basically a medieval building though it has been extensively restored in more recent times. Like many of the older Welsh churches, St John's has a simple bell-cote in place of a tower. In the mid-nineteenth century three new churches were built within ten years. One of these, St Elvan, makes a fine landmark in the centre of the town, with its tall needle-like spire. Aberdare also has a number of good chapels, although none is especially outstanding.

In the nineteenth century Aberdare was noted for the high standard of its cultural life and in particular for a famous choir, 'Cor Caradog'. The conductor of the choir, known affectionately as Caradog, but whose real name was Griffith Rhys Jones, became famous when he took the specially formed 456-strong choir to compete at the Crystal Palace, London, where they won the chief choral prize two years running in 1872 and 1873. After the conductor's death a public subscription was organised to provide a commemorative statue of Jones and this memorial was eventually erected in Victoria Square in front of the Black Lion Inn. Aberdare was also the birthplace of Alun Lewis, poet and short-story writer. He was killed at the age of 39 while on active service in India during the Second World War. As with the deaths of Hedd Wyn and Wilfred Owen in the First World War, the death of Lewis was one of the tragic losses to poetry this century.

Aberdare has always been fortunate to possess a fine park with its own boating lake. Today it is doubly fortunate for now there is also an excellent two-mile-long country park at the upper end of the Dâr valley. Formerly an area covered by coal tips and other unsightly scars of the Industrial Revolution, it has been transformed by careful land reclamation which includes re-routing parts of the river and the formation of lakes and a cascade, and tree planting. A variety of trails can be followed to explore either the historical development of coalmining in the area, or the course of the Afon Dar, from its source above the cliffs at the end of the park.

Of all the towns of the Valleys, Merthyr Tydfil is perhaps the most interesting. Not only is it the largest, but it is also the most historic and diverse in character. The mineral exploitation and industrial development of the district started in earnest more than two hundred years ago, giving rise to the rapidly expanding urban conglomeration which by the middle of the nineteenth century had become the metropolis of Wales. It was the chief centre of the iron industry in the early nineteenth century as well as being one of the first centres of Welsh non-conformity, the scene of the world's first steam locomotive and also the first constituency in Britain to return a Socialist MP to Westminster.

There had been a small iron furnace near Merthyr Tydfil as far back as the sixteenth century, but it was the coming of the great ironmasters in the latter part of the eighteenth century, together with the demand for munitions during the American Civil War, which transformed the town into the main industrial centre of the Valleys. By 1796 there were five ironworks in the district.

The famous Cyfarthfa Ironworks were started in 1766 and then taken over by Richard Crawshay of Yorkshire. By the turn of the century it employed 1,500 men and was the largest ironworks in Britain. Visitors to the works were invariably impressed by its sheer size and awestruck by its appearance, especially after dark when the sky was lit up by the red glow of the furnaces. Watkin George, 'the mechanical genius of Cyfarthfa', belongs to this early period of ironmaking. Starting as a village carpenter he rose to become a partner in the company and was responsible among other things for constructing a giant water-wheel and one of the first prefabricated iron bridges in the country. Very little now remains from the great Cyfarthfa Ironworks but Cyfarthfa Castle, the home of the Crawshay family, still stands in its own park on the northern outskirts of the town. Grandly conceived in medieval style, the 'castle', built in 1825, represented a reaction to the squalor and misery of industrialisation and was a nostalgic and romantic escape (for those who could afford it), back to another age. Much has changed since the days of the great ironmasters and Cyfarthfa Castle is now partly a museum and art gallery and partly a school. One of the delights of the art gallery is the collection of watercolour paintings by Penry Williams, a native of Merthyr and son of a stone mason. They show views from Cyfarthfa Castle of its surroundings, including the great ironworks, as they were in the early nineteenth century and should not be missed.

Another native of Merthyr was Joseph Parry, the musician. Born in 1841, he grew up amidst the Cyfarthfa Ironworks. By the time he was nine years old he was working in the coal pits and at twelve he was an iron worker. When he was 13 years old his family emigrated to the United States of America where he was able to study music in his spare time. His compositions were sent from America to the National Eisteddfod in Wales and aroused so much enthusiasm that a public fund was raised to enable him to return to Britain and study at the Royal Academy of Music in London. Eventually, he became the first professor of music at the new University of Wales, composed a number of operas and oratorios and amongst other works the beautiful hymn tune 'Aberystwyth'.

By the middle of the nineteenth century it was the turn of the Dowlais Ironworks, at the other end of Merthyr, to claim the distinction of being the largest ironworks in the world. It then had eighteen blast furnaces, employed 7,000 men and had become the first ironworks in Britain to make steel by the Bessemer process. The Dowlais Ironworks were owned by the Guest family and they also had a large mansion (now demolished) and park near the ironworks, but as ironmasters they appear to have been more philanthropic than the Crawshays. Both Sir John and Lady Charlotte Guest took a keen and active interest in the welfare of their workmen and early in the century they established a school in the upper floor of the handsome Dowlais Stables for the workmen's children. At this school, the children paid a penny or twopence a week, depending on their parents' circumstances. Later, Lady Charlotte had a more impressive Central School (with great Perpendicular windows) and the classical-style Memorial Library built in memory of her husband. Both buildings were designed by Sir Charles Barry, the architect of the Houses of Parliament. Lady Guest is chiefly remembered for her work in editing and partly translating into English the epic Welsh saga of *The Mabinogion*.

The Penydarren Ironworks were founded in 1784, almost next door to the Dowlais Ironworks, by the Homfray family. Compared to Cyfarthfa an Dowlais, it was always a relatively small ironworks yet Samuel Homfray, its manager, probably had a more profound effect on the history of southern Wales than either of the other ironmasters. In 1790 he was one of the chief promoters of a Bill for the construction of the Glamorganshire Canal from Merthyr Tydfil to Cardiff. The building of the canal between 1792 and 1794 was a tremendous achievement, involving the construction of 40 locks in a distance of 20 miles. It allowed iron to be transported efficiently to Cardiff for the first time. More significant even than the canal was Homfray's promotion in 1799 of a Bill for the Cardiff and Merthyr Railway. This received strong opposition from the Canal Company and the Bill had to be withdrawn, but as a compromise a nine-mile-long tramway was built instead between Merthyr and Abercynon where it joined with the canal. It was opened in 1800 as the Penydarren Tramroad. Four years later it was the scene of Richard Trevithick's trials with the world's first steam locomotive to run successfully on a railway. The engine hauled its five trucks, loaded with ten tons of iron and men at a speed of five miles per hour and won for Homfray a bet of a thousand guineas against Richard Crawshay.

Not all of Merthyr Tydfil's history has been connected with the iron and coal industry. The Romans, for example, had an auxiliary fort here at Penydarren in the latter part of the first century. Nothing, however, now remains to be seen of the Roman *castrum*, although fragmentary ruins have been found during excavations.

Far more remarkable are the ruins of the late thirteenth-century Morlais castle two miles north of the town centre. Its situation, more than 400 feet above the narrow Taf Fechan valley with superb views north towards the Brecon Beacons, is magnificent. Only fragments of towers and curtain walls remain now but they are sufficient for the layout of this redoubtable fortress to be made out clearly. The west curtain wall stands precariously at the edge of precipitous cliffs and the other sides are protected by an impressive rock-cut dry moat. The most interesting architectural feature of the castle is the circular keep-tower sited on the highest ground at the south-east corner. The upper part is completely ruined but the lower chamber, now half-buried amongst rubble from the upper storeys, is in near perfect condition. In the centre of the room there is a single column from which twelve gracefully arched ribs fan out, supporting the floor above and terminating in vertical pilasters on the perimeter wall. Such an unexpected architectural treasure at the summit of a deserted and windswept crag more than justifies the effort required to get there.

Morlais Castle was probably built in 1288 by Gilbert de Clare, Lord of Glamorgan, to guard the route from Brecon into the northernmost part of his lordship. The result of this show of force was a violent quarrel between de Clare and de Bohun, Lord of Brecon, which was only suppressed by the intervention of Edward I. In silencing the dispute Edward took advantage of his position as mediator to reduce the privileges of the Marcher barons, thus extending his control over the Welsh Marches. In June 1295 the King himself came to the castle at the end of his forced march from northern Wales, during the Third War of Welsh Independence.

Merthyr is more renowned for its non-conformity than its conformity in religious as well as other matters. By the middle of the seventeenth century it was already an important centre of Puritanism. The first dissenting congregation, reputed to have been the earliest in Wales, was formed about 1620 with a meeting-house at Blaen-canaid farm hidden away amongst the hills to the west of the town. By 1669 Merthyr was probably the greatest stronghold of dissenters in Wales, with between 300 and 600 people attending secret conventicles in the parish. Cwm-y-glo, the first permanent chapel, was a barn-like building erected in 1689 not far from Blaen-canaid. It survived until 1749, when its lease ran out and a new chapel was built instead in the town centre.

The Miners' Hall in Church Street was once a chapel before being taken over in 1921 and lengthened. Reputedly, it was designed by the great railway engineer, Isambard Kingdom Brunel to take the place of an earlier chapel which stood on the site of the railway station in High Street.

Until recently, the face of Merthyr Tydfil had hardly changed since the beginning of the nineteenth century. Now redevelopment is altering the appearance of huge areas of the town. Gone are the ironworks and all the mansions of the ironmasters, except the Crawshays' 'castle', and gone are many of the early terrace cottages of the miners and ironworkers. Gone, also, is the fortress-like market at Dowlais, the Central School, the Iron Bridge, the canal, the Penydarren tramroad, Brunel's railway station and his famous viaducts and also many of the best loved chapels. One hopes that eventually they will be replaced by something of real worth, for this was a historic, hard-working and vital town which had great character and which deserves something better than the humdrum architecture that can be seen in redevelopment schemes all over Britain.

The Heads of the Valleys road streaks eastwards from Merthyr across two superbly elegant bridges at Cefn-coed-y-cymmer and across the moorlands to Bryn-mawr, skirting on its way the old iron towns of Rhymni, Tredegar and Ebbw Vale. Rhymni still has the air of a town devastated by the sufferings of the depression in the inter-war years. Its famous Bute Ironworks, with blast furnaces designed to look like an Egyptian temple, have gone but the Company Shop still survives in a forlorn state. Lawn Shop, as the

Company Shop was known locally, gained a certain notoriety in the nineteenth century by its continuance of the truck system (whereby workmen were paid in goods rather than cash), some 54 years after it had been officially abolished by the Anti-Truck Act of 1831. An entertaining account of the shop and the development of the town was written by Dr Thomas Jones, one of Rhymni's more enlightened sons. From humble beginnings, he became a brilliant Civil Servant, adviser to four Prime Ministers, founded Coleg Harlech and eventually became President of the University College at Aberystwyth.

Tredegar also had a famous son who started life in humble surroundings. This was Aneurin Bevan, a fiercely independent socialist, who is now remembered as the founder of the National Health Service. A forerunner of the National Health Service was Tredegar's own Medical Aid Society which had functioned successfully since about 1915. One of the doctors employed by the Medical Aid Society was the Scottish author A. J. Cronin. His novel, *The Citadel*, was partly based on his experiences as a young doctor in Tredegar where he first went into practice.

The most notable architectural feature of Tredegar is the way in which the streets of the old town centre radiate from a circular *piazza*, apparently an early example of industrial town planning. An iron clock tower, 72 feet high, stands in the middle of the circle. This was erected in 1858, partly from the proceeds of a bazaar, for no particular reason except to ornament the town.

North of Tredegar a narrow road leads to the quarrying village of Trefil and on to Mynydd Llangynidr. Just beyond Trefil is the Duke's Table, a circular mound close to a cool spring, reputedly constructed as a place for the Duke of Beaufort to stop and picnic when out hunting. The road eventually dwindles to a track which follows the course of the old Bryn Oer Tramroad around the steep end of Dyffryn Crawnon – a beautiful example of a glaciated valley – and over the hills to the Brecon Canal at Tal-y-bont. The tramroad was constructed in 1815 to take iron and coal from the Valleys to Brecon and to bring back timber from the Usk valley and limestone from the Trefil quarries to the collieries and ironworks. By 1865 the tramroad had been abandoned. Now, more than a century later, it makes an excellent footpath for exploring some of the lesser known foothills of the Brecon Beacons. A large twin-chambered cave near the top of Mynydd Llangynidr, known as the Chartist Cave, was the refuge for John Frost and his fellow Chartists in 1838, while planning their revolutionary march on Newport.

Ebbw Vale has been a more flourishing town than Tredegar since the Second World War but is environmentally less attractive. The lower part of the town is dominated by the massive steelworks built just before the War on the site of the old ironworks. It is thus the only Valley town to have retained a direct link with the iron industry. Ebbw Vale's red sandstone church of St David is one of the best of the nineteenth-century valley churches.

Bryn-mawr, standing at almost 1,200 feet above sea level, can claim the distinction of being the highest town in the British Isles. Nearby in Cwm Clydach is Fairy Glen, a delightful miniature gorge.

From Bryn-mawr the main road back to the sea and Newport goes down the Ebbw Fach valley past Nanty-y-glo, another place famous in the nineteenth century for its great ironworks. In the 1830's the district seethed with unrest and bands of men with blackened faces known as 'Scotch Cattle', because of the animal horns which they sometimes wore, roamed the hills, forcibly trying to make everyone accept the workers' unions. Even the Crawshay Bailey family, for all their wealth and power as the ironmasters of Nant-y-glo, were frightened and had to take measures to ensure their own safety. Behind their mansion they built two fortified towers of iron and stone and stocked them for times of emergency. Curiously, the two circular towers still stand, albeit in a partly ruined state, but Nant-y-glo House, the ironmaster's mansion, has been demolished.

Three miles away, over the hill at Blaenafon, are the extensive ruins of one of the earliest of the Welsh ironworks. The Blaenafon Ironworks were started in 1790. Now it is the only site which gives any idea of what an early ironworks looked like and is gradually being transformed into an industrial museum. When complete the museum will include restored blast furnaces, a cast tower, a water balance tower and a block of workmen's cottages. It is very appropriate that these ironworks should be preserved, for it was here in 1878 that Sidney Thomas, at the age of 27, helped by his cousin Peter Gilchrist, carried out successful experiments for removing phosphorus from pig-iron in order to make fine steel. The discovery revolutionised the steel industry everywhere. Ironically, the experiments which were to make the world richer and led to the growth of the great German steel industry, only made Blaenafon poorer in comparison. Andrew Carnegie bought the formula, but Thomas was only able to enjoy the fortune from his invention for a short while for he was in poor health and seven years later he died in Paris at the age of 35.

Gradually, the heavy industries out of which the valley townships were born have given way to lighter and more diversified industries and consequently the Valleys have been able to find a new lease of life. Gradually, too, the Valleys are at last waking up to their environmental potential, though ironically it sometimes needs a terrible disaster, such as the horrific tragedy at Aberfan (where 116 schoolchildren were buried alive in 1966 when their school was engulfed by a coal-tip avalanche), before action is taken. Now a tip has been removed here, another tip afforested there and old ironworks and collieries have been cleared. From the ashes new sources of inspiration and recreation have risen, such as the country park at Aberdare, the industrial museum at Blaenafon and the forest park with scenic drives at Aber-carn.

The last-mentioned amenity is an excellent place to end a tour of the Valleys. The forest starts at the edge of the mining town and through it a seven-mile-long scenic drive skirts up and down the sides of the beautiful Nant Carn valley. Along the way there are picnic places, hairpin bends, a delightful grotto and idyllic views of the forest and valley. Near the top one can leave the car at a car park and walk up to the bare summit of Twmbarlwm crowned by the multiple ramparts of its Iron-Age hill-fort. From the top the prospect is superb – in front, Newport lies spread out across the coastal plain with the Severn Sea beyond and England in the distance; behind Twmbarlwm are the mountains of Gwent and Glamorgan and on the horizon are the peaks of the Brecon Beacons.

CHAPTER FOUR

Gwent

The land of Gwent originally comprised the area between the rivers Wye and Usk. After the Act of Union of Wales and England in the sixteenth century Gwynllwg, lying to the west of Gwent between the Afon Llwyd and the Afon Rhymni, was added to the former to become the county of Monmouthshire. Now, since 1974, the old name of Gwent has been revived although the boundaries of the county have hardly been affected.

The modern name Wentllwg (or Wentlloog), for the low-lying area between Cardiff and Newport appears at first to be a derivation of the name Gwent but is in actual fact a bastardised version of Gwynllwg. But just as the name is deceptive so is the countryside itself. At first glance one can hardly believe that this is part of Wales for the desolate reclaimed marshland is absolutely flat and virtually at sea level. Indeed, it seems to belong more to the fenlands north of Cambridge and conjures up the same kind of mysterious atmosphere. As in the Fens, great earthen banks protect Wentllwg from flooding by the sea and the land itself is drained by a network of straight dykes or reens. Even the churches here bear a superficial resemblence to the splendid edifices of the Fens, being largely Perpendicular Gothic in style and exotic in comparison to the humble churches of the hills to the north. Best of all is St Peter's church at Peterston-Wentllwg with its Somerset-type tower, similar in appearance but less ornate and more rustic, to those at Llandaf Cathedral and St Johns, Cardiff. St Brides Church, further along the coast, has the same kind of tower and like St Peter's has a tablet commemorating the "Great Flud of 20 Januarie 10 in the morning of 1606". The flood submerged 24 parishes in the coastal strip

between Cardiff and Chepstow and was reported as being the worst inundation since the time of Noah! Nearly all the churches in the area have plaques recording the event and the level of the flood.

The entrance to Newport is graced by Tredegar Park and its magnificent mansion, the largest Renaissance house in Wales. Though until recently used as a Roman Catholic school the house is now open to the public and is well worth a visit to see its lavishly decorated rooms. In the mid-sixteenth century it was described as "a very faire place of stone" and part of the Tudor building is incorporated in the Renaissance mansion built a century later in red brick. The previous owners of the house were the Morgan family of whom Godfrey Charles Morgan, Viscount Tredegar, was the most illustrious member. At the age of 24 he took part in the memorable 'Charge of the Light Brigade' at Balaclava in 1854 and came out of the action with only 32 men in the regiment after starting off the same morning with 145 men. The large park which still surrounds the mansion is now only a fraction of its former extent. At one time the park extended north to Bassaleg and included Gwern y Clepa, the home of Ifor Hael (one of the ancestors of the Morgan family). In the fourteenth century Ifor Hael, renowned for his generous nature, was reputed to have been the chief patron of Wales' most famous bard, the Ceredigion poet Dafydd ap Gwilym. It is, perhaps, difficult now to associate this part of Gwent with Welsh poetry, but in Ifor Hael's time, and for many centuries afterwards, Welsh was virtually the only language spoken in the area.

Newport is not a particularly beautiful town, though like Cardiff it grew rich on the wealth of the Valleys. Nevertheless, it has a number of places of interest. For instance, right in the centre, alongside the Usk river and next to the railway station, are the towers and walls of Newport Castle, a fourteenth-century stone fortress squashed incongruously between river and road and two bridges. St Woollos, formerly the parish church but since 1921 the cathedral of the Monmouth diocese, stands on Stow Hill at the other end of the town. An oddly elongated building from the outside, it has inside a fine twelfth-century nave entered through a richly decorated Romanesque arch. In the centre of the town in

High Street, Murenger House – an Elizabethan half-timbered building – has survived from as far back as 1541 and is now a restaurant. Above the town centre stands the monumental but curiously un-classical looking Civic Centre, its tall central tower completed almost 30 years after the start of construction in 1937. Inside there are colourful murals depicting the life and history of the county.

The best known of Newport's buildings is the unusual transporter bridge near the Docks. Built in 1902 by the French engineer Arnodin it is really a high-suspension bridge supported on deceptively slender pylons which taper to points at their bases. Suspended from the main span a travelling carriage hovers above the Usk and transports vehicles and people across the river. This was one of the finest of a number of similar bridges built in different parts of the world during the early part of the century; most have now been dismantled, leaving the Newport bridge as almost the last example.

Buildings, however, are of secondary importance in Newport's history. One of its chief claims to fame is the Chartist Riot of 1839 when disillusioned workers from the Valleys north of Newport banded together on a stormy November night and marched into the town in support of their demands for constitutional reform. The authorities were prepared for them and when they halted in front of the Westgate Hotel there was a scuffle. Immediately troops in the hotel opened fire, killing several of the demonstrators. The leaders of the Chartists, including John Frost, a former mayor of Newport, were arrested and condemned to death, but this sentence was eventually changed to transportation to Australia.

Newport's other claim to fame is W. H. Davies, poet and super-tramp. He was born in the docks end of the town in 1871 and is perhaps best known for his countryside poems. Yet despite his nostalgia for the green villages of Gwent and his love of nature – 'What is this life if, full of care, we have no time to stand and stare' – he had a sardonic streak, particularly when referring to the Welsh, perhaps as a result of a birching he once received at Newport Gaol for petty thieving. He had the wandering spirit of the bardic harpmen of old and in 1893 sailed to America, spending five years tramping around there before losing a leg when trying to jump a goods train. He returned to Britain and spent the next six years living in doss-houses in Newport and London on a legacy of eight shillings a week and desperately trying to save up money to publish his poems. Eventually his first volume of verse was published in 1905. This was followed in 1908 by his famous *Autobiography of a Supertramp*, in which he described his adventures on the road, and by a prodigious outpouring of 749 poems.

To Davies, Llantarnam, Magor, Malpas, Llanwern, Liswery, old Caerleon and Allt yr Yn were 'the villages so green'. Today Llanwern has been overwhelmed by an enormous steelworks and all the other places, apart from Magor and Caerleon, have been overrun by encroachments of Newport and the new town of Cwm-brân. Caerleon, though so near to Newport, still stands physically aloof and appropriately so, for it has a far longer history. Caerleon's beginnings go back, in fact, to the first century AD when the Romans established a fortress there. Known to the Romans as Isca it was one of two legionary fortresses, (the other being at Chester in the north), that they founded to control the routes into Wales. For two centuries Isca was the permanent base of the Second Augusta Legion until the fortress was superseded by the one at Cardiff. Today Isca is largely covered by later buildings and though large parts have been excavated by archaeologists, thus revealing the layout in considerable detail, little can be seen above ground save for one of the barrack blocks which has been preserved. Most of the finds from the excavations are now kept in the Caerleon Legionary Museum near the parish church. Immediately outside the fortress walls, however, is one of the most impressive monuments of Roman Britain. This is the amphitheatre, a great open arena encircled by stone walls and earthen banks which once held tiered seating for 6,000 spectators. The amphitheatre was built mainly as a training ground for the soldiers but occasionally it was used for sports and public displays. If, in fact, Julius and Aaron, the first Christians known by name in Wales, were sacrificed at Caerleon as reported at the threshold of the fourth century then it was probably this amphitheatre that was the scene of their martyrdom.

A few miles further east at Caer-went the Romans built Venta Silurum, a civil town designed to a rectangular layout in a similar manner to that of their forts. On three sides of the town the Roman walls with their semi-octagonal towers still stand and are clearly visible but, as at Caerleon, later building has covered much of the interior although the remains of a small temple and two shops have been exposed. The main road through Caer-went lies above the Roman road which went from the east gate, of which fragments still remain, to the west gate and was two to three times as wide as the modern street. In the porch of the parish church (on the site of the Roman public baths) two fine Roman inscribed stones have been preserved. One of these, probably from the base of a statue, is dedicated to the commander of the second Augusta Legion by decree of the senate of the Silures.

Venta Silurum was the administrative centre of the Silures during Roman times, having been established by the conquerors, as was their custom in other parts of Britain and Gaul, to replace the tribes' former hill-fort capital and to persuade the native inhabitants to adopt Roman ways of life and behaviour. Traces of the Silures' old capital can still be seen in the banks and ditches of Llanmelin hill-fort a mile north of Caer-went. Though Caer-went itself became deserted after the departure of the Romans their influence was not entirely negative. It would indeed have been surprising if everything had been forgotten for the Celts had become intensely Romano-British in spirit, as can be seen by the way Christianity was able to flourish in Wales during the dark centuries which followed the Roman departure. It is also significant that the Welsh language – the only living language directly evolved from the British tongue – still retains many of the Latin roots by which it was enriched.

While Caer-went has remained almost unchanged for the last hundred years or more Caldicot, a mile to the south, has recently mushroomed into a small town. Fortunately, this has not disturbed the peaceful parkland setting of Caldicot Castle on the east side of the town. The moat which surrounded the castle is now dry, but much else remains including a great round keep-tower at one corner. The castle's main attraction now is the nightly medieval banquet which is held in delightful surroundings to the accompaniment of traditional Welsh singing and harp music.

Caldicot Level, like Wentllwg Level between Cardiff and Newport is another flat, low-lying area of reclaimed marshland and is also protected from periodic flooding by a great earthen bank or sea-wall. It is not known when the sea-wall was first built, but it is probably of Roman origin for only the Roman legions would have had sufficient labour to undertake such an enormous task. There is evidence too of Roman involvement from the centurial stone, recording work done on the sea-wall, which was washed away in 1878 at Goldcliff, near Newport, and is now in the museum at Caerleon.

The easternmost town in Gwent is Chepstow near the mouth of the Wye. Alongside the Wye, which here forms a clearcut and dramatic boundary between Wales and England, stands Chepstow Castle, built on a spectacular site between the high limestone cliffs of the river on one side and a deep ravine on the other. This was the first of the Norman castles to be erected on the Welsh side of Offa's Dyke. Because of its great strategic importance the keep was built from the start in stone instead of the usual timber. Continual wars necessitated constant rebuilding and enlargement until the whole of the long narrow ridge was covered with a magnificent array of rectangular and circular towers linked by lofty curtain walls, all perched on the edge of precipitous cliffs.

A large part of the thirteenth-century town wall surrounding Chepstow still stands in good condition, particularly between High Street and the railway line. High Street itself is spanned by the Gothic arch of the sixteenth-century West Gate where, in days gone by, the merchants paid their tolls to the Lord of the Manor for goods brought into the town.

Inside the town walls, Cheptow is a busy and lively place with all its streets descending steeply down the hill towards the river and John Rennie's elegant five-arch iron bridge. The parish church, originally a Benedictine priory, was largely rebuilt in the nineteenth century, but still retains a fine Romanesque doorway and window on the west front.

North of Chepstow the main road leaves the Wye behind for a

while, but after passing the largest racecourse in Wales at Piercefield Park it returns towards the river. At Wyndcliff there is a marvellous view below of the Wye as it makes one of its long, slow loops, this time around tiny Lancaut and its ruined church. The valley is filled with trees and beyond the river, in the middle distance, is a long line of white limestone cliffs at Wintours Leap and in the far distance the Severn. The road then continues northwards, following the winding river as closely as possible through beautiful but more subdued scenery to Tintern and Monmouth.

Tintern Abbey is the jewel of the Wye Valley. Though roofless for four centuries most of the walls of the abbey still remain to eaves level. At either end of the nave and presbytery are great wall-wide windows still filled with stone tracery and perhaps more striking in decay than when they were covered with dark stained glass. One can easily imagine that in the moonlight the ruins are, as one early writer put it, 'indescribably fine and solemnly grand'. Few of the monastic quarters around the church still stand but their layout can be easily seen from the exposed foundations and low walls.

In the late eighteenth century when tourists first began to appreciate the wilder parts of Britain, Monmouth was one of the earlier centres of exploration. The name Monmouth is derived from Mynwy, the Welsh name for the Monnow river which joins the Wye here, and is still pronounced west of the Usk as 'Munmuth'. It is a delightful town with an unexpected grace and some fine buildings. Pride of place goes to the Monnow Bridge with its medieval gateway astride the roadway. This is the only fortified bridge gateway in Britain and one of the few remaining in Europe. Then there are the remains of Monmouth Castle on a bank overlooking the Monnow river. Within the castle's precincts is the Great Castle House, built in 1873, for the third Marquis of Worcester. The mansion is beautifully proportioned and quietly dignified from the outside, while inside it has fine woodwork and superbly decorated plaster ceilings.

Just below the castle, in Agincourt Square, is the stately eighteenth-century Shire Hall. A niche in the wall of the Shire Hall contains a larger-than-life-size statue of Henry V, a reminder that he was born in Monmouth Castle in 1387. At the battle of Agincourt much of Henry V's success was due to his countrymen, the bowmen of Gwent, who with their superior skill with the longbow outclassed all other bowmen.

More renowned, possibly, than Henry of Monmouth was Geoffrey of Monmouth, the twelfth-century cleric who wrote the epic *History of the Kings of Britain* and in doing so laid down the foundations of the great Arthurian legend that spread across Europe and was to be retold in different ways countless times for centuries afterwards. According to Geoffrey, his *History* was translated from a 'a certain ancient book written in the British language', presumably Welsh, but no one has yet been able to identify the source or sources with certainty. There is even doubt that there was an earlier source, for Geoffrey's book is little more than fiction within a historical framework partly based on ancient British legends. Geoffrey's motive in writing such a work is also obscure, although in part it seems to have been a patriotic one intended to prove to the Normans that they had conquered a great kingdom with a noble heritage. Whatever the reasons the *History* was popular everywhere, but nowhere more than in Wales for in spite of Geoffrey's somewhat contemptuous attitude to the Welsh of his own day, he had given them the most noble descent in Europe, a line which went back more than two thousand years to the mythical Brutus, great grandson of the Trojan Aeneas.

Another famous son of Monmouth was Charles Stewart Rolls, the pioneer of aviation and motoring and a co-founder of Rolls-Royce Ltd. He was also to be one of the first British victims of a flying accident when the tail of his aeroplane collapsed over Bournemouth in 1910. A bronze statue of Rolls stands in front of the Shire Hall and there are memorabilia of the man in the local museum. Also in the museum are interesting relics relating to Lord Nelson who, with Lady Hamilton visited the town in 1802.

Monmouth has two churches, one of which, St Thomas's, still has considerable Romanesque work, and a public school, founded as far back as 1614 and rebuilt in 1864. More interesting than these, however, is the hill just outside the town, called the Kymin. Here, on the top, are two unusual follies erected at the turn of the eighteenth century. The Round House was built in 1794 as a place where "the first gentlemen of Monmouth" could hold meetings and dine in luxury while admiring the views across the Wye Valley. The Naval Temple was erected six years later in order to perpetuate the names of eighteenth-century admirals. Medallions on the frieze below the roof commemorate 15 admirals, including Nelson who breakfasted here in style on his visit to Monmouth, but the statue of Britannia which once crowned the temple has gone.

Monmouth was of such strategic importance to the early invaders that three castles, known as 'The Trilateral', were built to defend it on the northern and western approaches at Skenfrith, Grosmont and near Llantilio Crossenny. Each of these villages also has interesting churches which are well worth visiting, particularly that at Grosmont which was built on an unusually large scale with an octagonal tower and spire.

The trilateral castles, fine though they are, are completely eclipsed in scale by Raglan Castle standing just north of the A40 road halfway between Monmouth and Abergavenny. Raglan Castle was virtually the last fortress to be built in Wales until the eighteenth century and with it the long era of castle building came to a magnificent end. There had been a castle there since Norman times, but in the mid-fifteenth century it was rebuilt not as a defence against bows and arrows but to withstand cannon fire. In addition, there were sumptuous apartments around a double courtyard, for it was intended for luxurious living as well as defence. There is a remarkable hexagonal tower (known as the Yellow Tower of Gwent) surrounded by gun turrets and a wide moat so that in the event of a siege it could be held independently of the rest of the castle. All this was to be of no avail, however, for in 1646 after an eleven-week siege Raglan was forced to surrender to the Parliamentarians and the Yellow Tower, though unscathed by the battles, was mined and partly destroyed to prevent its further use. The fall of Raglan Castle marked the effective end of the first Civil War.

In a county so full of genuine castles as Gwent it might seem to be an act of perverse frivolity to erect a sham castle, yet only three miles from Raglan there is a worthy example, complete with boldly castellated towers, that was built for the most serious of reasons. According to a plaque on the wall of Clytha Castle the folly was built by William Jones in 1790 in order 'to relieve a mind sincerely afflicted by the loss of a most excellent wife'. No pains were spared in building this touching tribute to Elisabeth Jones for, if her gravestone in Llanarth churchyard is anything to go by, she must have been a paragon with virtues that included 'every hereditary virtue of the House of Cavendish, Purity and Innocence itself', and 'a most extensive Genius'. Clytha House on the opposite side of the road is a mid-nineteenth century rebuilding in classical style, but the Gothic gateway through which the grounds are entered dates from the same time as the 'castle'.

Nearby and on either side of the Usk river are two interesting churches at Bettws Newydd and Llanfair Cilgedin. Bettws church has one of those delicately designed and superbly carved timber rood-screens that are found in a number of churches along the Welsh border. Llanfair church is unusual for the incised *graffito* work (carried out in 1888) which completely covers all the walls inside.

A couple of miles further west is Llanover House where in the nineteenth century lived Lady Llanover, a woman remarkable for her championship of the Welsh language and customs and for buying local inns and converting them into coffee houses. She was an ardent supporter of local *eisteddfodau* and it was she more than anyone else who revived the so-called national costumes of Wales by sketching and painting them, by dressing her household staff in them and by herself wearing the warm woollens that she advocated. Of course there never was such a thing as a 'national' costume in Wales any more than in any other part of Britain, or even most parts of Western Europe for that matter, but only peasant costumes which varied considerably and were not confined to particular localities. Nevertheless, such was Lady Llanover's zeal that she had little difficulty in convincing people that there was a national costume and in persuading her friends to wear it on public occasions. In her husband, Sir Benjamin Hall, she found a willing supporter for her ideals. He was also something of a reformer himself in parliamentary and local government circles and gave his name to 'Big Ben' in the Westminster parliament building.

Abergavenny, lying where the Gafenni joins the Usk and encircled by hills and mountains, has one of the most pleasant sites of any town in Wales. For centuries it has been the gateway to the west, holding the key to the upper Usk valley where the Usk river passes down from the Brecon Beacons between the high shoulders of the Sugar Loaf and Blorenge mountains. The Romans may have been the first to fortify the site, but there are no remains now of the fort which they built; it may lie under the remains of the Norman castle standing on a bluff south of the town. There is a walk around the outside of the castle with good views across the Vale of Usk to Blorenge and nearby there is an interesting museum.

Abergavenny's pride is the parish church of St Mary. It was originally the chapel of a Benedictine priory founded in the eleventh or early twelfth century and this accounts for its great length which was necessary to accommodate both parishioners and monks. The west front and part of the nave is a nineteenth-century rebuild, but the rest of the church, including the massive fortress-like tower, is medieval. Inside, the church has somehow, despite wars and restorations, managed to retain a splendid set of fourteenth-century choir stalls. There are also some excellent tombs in the Herbert and Lewis Chapels. The oldest tomb, that of Eva de Braose (died 1246) is a reminder of an earlier member of the family, namely the notorious William de Braose, Lord of Abergavenny and perpetrator of foul deeds against the Welsh and his family. One Christmas he invited 70 Welshmen to feast at the castle and then had them murdered in cold blood as they celebrated; on another occasion he left his wife and son to starve to death at the murderous hands of King John while he escaped to France after quarrelling with the monarch over money matters.

At one time Abergavenny was a celebrated centre for Welsh flannel and the manufacture of periwigs made from goats' hair. These industries have long since disappeared and now, apart from the two large hospitals on the outskirts of the town, Abergavenny is mainly a market centre and dormitory town for the Valleys. Attractive and flourishing, it still lives up to George Owen's description of 1602: ' a fine town, wealthy and thriving'.

The most attractive thing about Abergavenny, however, is its exquisite site in a sort of amphitheatre formed by the hills and mountains on all sides. To the east is the little tree-clad hill of Ysgyryd Fach. To the north-east is Ysgyryd Fawr (Great Skirrid), an isolated hogsback in National Trust ownership. Though not as high as the other mountains in the vicinity, it has a wild appearance accentuated by a 300-foot chasm on one side which gives the mountain its Welsh name. The alternative name of 'Holy Mountain' also relates to this unusual feature for local tradition claims that the mountain was split at the time of the Crucifixion when 'the earth did quake and the rocks rent'. The little chapel of St Michael which once stood on the summit has disappeared almost entirely, but the ridge is still worth climbing for the fine views of the Black Mountains and the English border counties.

The rounded bulk of Blorenge (1,833 feet) rises steeply up on the south-west side of Abergavenny. For the energetic the most rewarding climb starts at the canal near Llanfoist and continues either through the woods and up the steep northern face or along the lanes and footpath to the south-east and up through the rounded *cwm* known as the Punchbowl. An easier route is by the road which leaves Govilon, where the first Baptist Chapel in Wales (1650) still stands, and then skirts the western side of the mountain.

Mynydd Pen-y-fal, or the Sugar Loaf, (1,955 feet) is deservedly the most popular mountain in the area for not only is it the highest but it is also the most shapely and the wildest in appearance. Virtually the whole of the mountain is in National Trust ownership and there is a variety of routes to the top, either by way of the three finger-like spurs that almost reach into Abergavenny's outskirts or from the Grwyne valley to the west and north. The summit itself is a long, narrow and surprisingly rocky ridge.

The long parallel ridges and valleys of the Black Mountains north of the Sugar Loaf and Abergavenny are divided among three counties, Powys, Gwent and Herefordshire. The middle part, incorporating the beautiful Honddu valley, is the most easily accessible from Abergavenny and belongs to Gwent, although like the valleys to the west of it is also part of the Brecon Beacons National Park. The secondary road through the Honddu valley leaves the main road at Llanfihangel Crucornau where there is a picturesque and ancient inn, the Skirrid Mountain Inn, that has associations with Judge Jeffreys and still retains the air of a coaching hostelry. Llanfihangel Court stands in its own grounds opposite the church and is interesting for the way in which it illustrates changing tastes. It was first built in the fifteenth century, but in 1559, when conditions were more peaceful, its front was rebuilt and extended to give a dignified symmetrical appearance conforming to the Renaissance fashion then beginning to make headway in Wales. The elaborate plaster ceilings inside were probably added still later in the seventeenth century.

Two miles up the Honddu valley, or Vale of Ewias as it is otherwise known, the scarred and contorted surface of Hatteral Mountain (on the right-hand side) appears out of character with the arcadian loveliness of the rest of the valley. Like the chasm on the face of Ysgyryd Fawr it is evidence of earth movements and landslips in earlier times. Some, at least, of the movements have taken place within historic times, and have made Cwmyoy church with its tilting tower and crooked walls a curiosity that seems only just able to hang on to its perch on the side of the mountain.

Four miles further on one comes to the stark ruin of Llanthony Abbey situated in a delectable setting that Giraldus Cambrensis (writing in 1188) though it was 'truly calculated for religion, and more adapted to canonical discipline than all the monasteries of the British Isles'. What Giraldus saw was an uncompleted Norman abbey with narrow roundheaded window to the central tower. At the beginning of the thirteenth century the church was completed by the addition of the nave and twin western towers (thus making it the only Welsh church with three towers), which by now had become transitional Gothic in architectural style, combining pointed arches alongside round-headed windows. At the end of the eighteenth century the south-west tower was converted to a shooting box and the prior's house adjoining it made into a house for his steward by Colonel Wood of Brecon. In 1807 the eccentric and poet, Walter Savage Landor, bought the estate with the intention of founding an ideal community. The idea was short-lived, for after starting improvements, importing sheep from

Spain and marrying, Landor quarrelled with his neighbours and left. The prior's house later became an hotel.

The ideal community did come a little later, but a few miles further upstream at the extreme end of the valley at Capel-y-ffin. Here, in 1870, Father Ignatius founded his own unorthodox version of a Benedictine monastery. The brick-built monastery which he started was never completed and after his death in 1908 it began to fall into ruins. In 1924 it became for a few years the home of the sculptor Eric Gill and his family and of David Jones, the artist. Some of their work still survives in the Chapel that Gill created out of the ruins, and in the refectory.

From Capel-y-ffin there is a choice of routes across the northern escarpment of the Black Mountains, either by road through the Gospel Pass (1,778 feet) to Hay or by bridleway over the Twmpa (2,263 feet) to Three Cocks and Talgarth. Both routes give superb views of the upper Wye Valley and much of mid-Wales.

CHAPTER FIVE

Brecon Beacons National Park

Although on the edge of a densely populated area and nearer to London than any other national park in Britain, the Brecon Beacons National Park is undeservedly the least well known of the three national parks in Wales. The Brecon Beacons cannot compare in grandeur with the rocky and historically symbolic vastness of Snowdonia in the north, or in dramatic qualities with the sea cliffs of the Pembrokeshire Coast in the west, but for sheer pastoral beauty they are unsurpassable. The mountains of the Brecon Beacons National Park do, indeed, have precipices and cliffs but unlike the Alpine crags of the north they do not dominate the scene; rather, they are highlights in a splendid panoramic landscape of luxuriant valleys and softly rounded peaks and ridges. Added to the apparent gentleness of the mountains (at least when viewed from below) is the genial loveliness of the valleys themselves with their lush tree planting, warm stone buildings and rich red-brown ploughed fields. Together the gentle shapes and warm colours have created a unique landscape that is richly attractive and human.

And yet for all their apparent mildness the uplands never look like mere hills – they are mountains good and proper, rising to almost 3,000 feet above sea level, with large expanses of bare wilderness, long lines of escarpments and remote corrie lakes all of which can be dangerous to the unwary. Like all real mountains, they should always be treated with respect and caution.

From Abergavenny in the east to Llandeilo in the west there are four main mountain ranges. They are the Black Mountains, the Brecon Beacons, Fforest Fawr and Y Mynydd Du. From their northern summits long ridges sweep grandly away to the southern boundary of the park where a narrow rim of limestone gives rise to some of the most fascinating scenery in the park. Here, on the very borders of the coalfield are picturesque waterfalls, towering gorges, craggy outcrops and vast cave systems.

The river valleys vary considerably, from the geologically young V-shaped valleys to the distinctive U-shaped glaciated valleys. Each is delightful, but surpassing all is the Usk valley crossing the park from west to east. Starting on the northern slopes of Y Mynydd Du the Usk river turns east along a beautiful valley to Brecon and then veers south-eastwards, paralleled by a canal, in a trench-like vale between the Brecon Beacons and the Black Mountains down to Crickhowell.

Crickhowell is delightfully situated on the east side of the Usk, cradled between the Old Red Sandstone slopes of the Black Mountains and the limestone cliffs of Mynydd Llangatwg. Its most prominent feature is the pretty broach spire of the fourteenth-century church on the western edge of the town. Just beyond the church and on a corner where the two main roads meet is Porth Mawr, a medieval castellated gateway which once formed the entrance to a Tudor mansion long since demolished. In a small park on the other side of the town the fragmentary remains of a castle bear witness to Owain Glyndŵr's war of independence at the beginning of the fifteenth century. In the more peaceful centuries that followed, Crickhowell became an important centre of the flannel industry and later still it acquired a good collection of Georgian houses.

In the early years of the nineteenth century Crickhowell became the home of Thomas Price for nearly 30 years. One of the foremost Celtic scholars of the day, Price was noted as a historian and antiquary. He did much to make the Welsh and the Bretons in France aware of their kinship and was largely instrumental in getting the Bible translated into Breton. As an ardent advocate of the language and culture of Wales he successfully established, as far back as 1820, a Welsh school in the district and also set up a school for blind harpists in Brecon.

Crickhowell was also the home of Sir George Everest, the

69

Surveyor General of India after whom Mount Everest was named. Gwern-vale, the mansion where Everest lived, still stands on the hillside above the Brecon road.

A lovely 13-arch, seventeenth-century bridge spans the Usk and connects Crickhowell to Llangatwg (Llangattock) on the west side of the river. Llangatwg crawls up the hill towards a delightful stretch of the Brecon Canal which here winds lazily around the base of the mountains. At the lower end of the village there is a massively towered church and inside this the old village stocks and whipping post can still be seen.

In the little valley beyond Llangatwg the great limestone cliffs of Craig y Cilau rise up like a miniature Grand Canyon. Here, amongst the rocky clefts, is one of the habitats of the Lesser Whitebeam, an indigenous plant related to the mountain ash and not known anywhere outside the Brecon Beacons National Park. Craig y Cilau is also caving country. The mountain behind the cliffs is honeycombed with a network of caverns, passages, and underground watercourses that includes some of the longest cave systems in the British Isles. Ogof Agen Allwedd (Keyhole Cave), for instance, was first discovered in 1948 and has now been explored for a length of 13 miles underneath Mynydd Llangatwg. Most of the caves are difficult to locate and are accessible only to experienced cavers but Ogof Eglwys Faen (Stone Church), halfway along the base of the cliffs, is fairly easy to find and has free access.

Many of the ridges and valleys of the Black Mountains can be reached most easily from Crickhowell. The nearest peak is Pen Cerig-calch (2,302 feet), two and a half miles away. Its summit is an isolated limestone cap which represents the last remnant of the vast limestone sheet which in prehistoric times must have lain right across the Usk valley and the Black Mountains. On a shoulder of the mountain are the oval ramparts of Crucywel hill-fort (after which Crickhowell gets its name). Beyond Pen Cerig-calch there is a marvellous ridge walk where one can walk northwards for nine miles without going below the 2,000-foot contour.

Patrisio church, buried deep in the hills above the Grwyne Fawr valley to the east of Crickhowell, is one of the rare monuments that have survived, almost by accident, virtually intact. Progress has

by-passed it and its very isolation has been the means of preserving its treasures. Without the aid of a good map it it is difficult to find, so snugly and delightfully is it hidden away in the folds of the valley, but it is well worth the effort to discover. Inside there is an eleventh-century font, a large number of wall murals including one with a skeletal figure of Death, and an oak cradle-roof. But the finest prize of this simple but enchanting little church is the exquisitely carved screen to the medieval rood-loft. Based on a restrained repetitive pattern the screen has the diffident charm and slender grace of delicate lace-work and one wonders how it could possibly have been fashioned by hand out of wood.

To the north of Crickhowell lies Tretŵr (Tretower) at the junction of two important routes, one to Brecon and the west via the pass of Bwlch and the other to Talgarth and the north via Pengenffordd pass. To control this strategic point between the Usk and Wye the Normans built a castle at the first opportunity. Originally a typical motte-and-bailey castle it was later rebuilt with a polygonal shell keep, but this was not sufficient to deter the Welsh and sometime about the end of the twelfth century it was overwhelmed and gutted. On regaining control the Anglo-Norman lord decided to rebuild again, but this time with a single round tower of massive proportions, and it is this great tower, rising up out of the earlier ruins, that can still be seen, standing alone amongst the flat meadows. By the mid-fifteenth century the conditions of life were somewhat quieter and the castle, which had now outlived its usefulness, was abandoned in favour of Tretower Court nearby. It was still necessary, however, take some protective measures and thus a large fortified gateway was built at the entrance to the courtyard of the mansion and linked to the stone and timber dwelling by a high-level wall-walk.

Nowhere, perhaps, was this desperate concern for defence more keenly felt than at the northern end of the gap between the Usk and Wye valleys. This was the route the invaders used to penetrate into mid-Wales and for centuries strife must have been part of the pattern of life. At Talgarth, sheltering in the northern foothills of the Black Mountains, there is a medieval tower-house (called simply Tower), a four-storey structure similar to the peel towers of the Scottish border but rarely found in Wales. Another tower-house still survives at Scethrog a few miles to the west. Not far away, the medieval mansion of Porth-aml Fawr (incidentally one of the many reputed resting places of Henry VII on his way to the Battle of Bosworth), has a detached and fortified gate-house. On the far side of the river and standing on a mound surrounded by trees is the thirteenth-century Bronllys castle which, like Tretŵr, now has a single round tower. Detached towers seem to have been the rage in this area for even the Norman church at Bronllys has a free-standing tower, possibly intended as a place of refuge.

Yet in spite of all this concern for defence Talgarth itself appears to have had a quiet existence undisturbed by military events. Of its two most eminent residents, one, Jane Williams, is now almost forgotten. She lived at Neuadd Felin in Church Street in the nineteenth century and during her lifetime was well known as the author of historical and biographical works about the *History of Wales, Literary Women of the Seventeenth Century*, and of Rev. Thomas Price (Carnhuanawc).

The other celebrity was Hywel Harris, one of the chief leaders of the Methodist Revival in Wales. He was born in 1714 at Trefeca Uchaf, a mile south-west of Talgarth. Harris was destined for the established church but his methods of preaching brought him into conflict with the local vicar and he soon became a Methodist. In 1752, after a quarrel with Daniel Rowland, another Methodist leader, the autocratic Harris founded a religious community at Trefeca based on the experiments of Moravians in England and Germany. The semi-monastic community aimed at a self-sufficient economy in which all members lived as a family, practising a large variety of crafts, woollen making and planned agriculture. The community was supported by the Countess of Huntingdon, and with her help a college for training young preachers was set up at Tredustan Court, nearby. This rich and pious lady became a widow after 18 years of marriage and devoted her 45 years of widowhood to founding a religious sect and building 64 chapels, in addition to supporting Harris in his work. After the death of Harris the community languished and the college was eventually taken over in 1842 by the Welsh Calvinistic Methodist Church. The

College closed in 1964 but a museum there devoted to the life and times of Harris is still open.

The road from Trefeca leads eventually to the little village of Llan-gors and Llan-gors Lake. Llyn Syfaddan, as the lake is known in Welsh, is a shallow stretch of water lying at the headwaters of the Afon Llyfni, five miles in circumference and thus the second largest natural lake in Wales. An excellent view of the lake and its surroundings can be had from the top of Mynydd Troed, a bare outlier of the Black Mountains just under 2,000 feet high. In the Middle Ages the lake was a sufficiently rich fishing ground to give rise to a Parliamentary survey in 1650 and was particularly renowned for the immense size of its fish which inspired the saying *'cyhyd a llyswen Syfaddan'* (as long as a Syfaddan eel). It is also rich in legends. It is reputed to be bottomless and the water of the Llynfi which flows through it on the way to join the Wye is said not to mix with that of the lake. Another legend (according to Giraldus Cambrensis) was that the birds sung of Gruffydd ap Rhys as being the rightful owner of the surrounding land and not the Norman invaders. Better known is the story of a submerged city, the walls and roofs of which it is said can be seen below the water in certain lighting conditions. This is probably a genuine relic of folk memory for the small island at the northern end was in fact inhabited in the distant past. In 1925 a *cafn unpren* (a dug-out canoe now in Brecon Museum), was found there, along with the remains of a prehistoric lake-dwelling which had been supported on wooden piles. In summertime the lake is busy with yachts and boats, but in winter it is deserted and becomes an important gathering ground for handsome Great Crested Grebes, and for Little Grebes, Goosanders, Herons and other wildfowl. It is also the most westerly limit of the pretty little Reed Warbler and the home of the now rare Medicinal Leech. The last Golden Eagle said to have been seen in southern Wales was reported fom Cathedin at the southern corner of the lake in the 1930's.

Cathedin was the home for a time of the playwright Christopher Fry who once lived at the Georgian-fronted house known as Trebinshwm. Nearby, at Llangasty Tal-y-llyn there is a delightfully designed group of buildings comprising a church, school and mansion. They were all built in 1849 in a fortified Tudor style for Robert Raikes of Gloucester, the founder of Sunday Schools, and are the work of J. L. Pearson.

At Bwlch, situated high up in a narrow col between the end of Mynydd Llan-gors and Buckland Hill, the secondary road meets the main Abergavenny to Brecon Road. On Buckland Hill Colonel Gwynne Holford, a veteran of Waterloo, undertook a novel form of memorial by planting a forest in which the lines of trees represented the ranks of infantry at the great battle.

Holford's own memorial is at Llansanffraed, a mile further north, in the church that he rebuilt in red sandstone in 1884. This is also the burial place of the religious poet Henry Vaughan, often known as the Silurist, and also as The Swan of Usk. He was born in 1610 at Newton, a farmhouse a little further along the road. After studying law at London and working for a time at Brecon, Vaughan turned his attention to medicine and returned to live at Newton. Here, beside the peaceful Usk which he dearly loved, he wrote his poetry, including the collection known as *Silex Scintillus*. After his wife's death Vaughan retired to a cottage at Scethrog a mile further upstream.

Tal-y-bont, on the opposite side of the Usk, is a good centre from which to explore the wild and beautiful country behind the Brecon Beacons. The hamlet stands at the side of the Monmouthshire and Brecon Canal (opened in 1801 and now one of the few Welsh canals still in use), and was in the nineteenth century the terminus of the old Bryn-oer tramroad that led across the mountains to the coalmining valleys. The site of the tramroad now makes a delightful footpath for walkers. For the Brecon Beacons themselves take the road westwards alongside Tal-y-bont reservoir and through beautiful Glyn Collwn between the arête-like ridge of Allt-lwyd (2,100 feet) and the shapely dome of Tory-y-foel. At the head of the valley there is a splendid waterfall (Blaen-y-Glyn) half-hidden in the woods and then the road climbs steeply up to the pass at Torpantau (1,446 feet high). From there the peaks of the Brecon Beacons can be approached by a fairly easy four-mile walk along the track of an old Roman road. Alternatively, one can continue on downhill to the Taf Fechan Forest and sample its delightful picnic places amongst the woodland glades or explore its interesting nature trails.

The road from Tal-y-bont to Brecon follows the canal past Pencelli and Llanfrynach. At Pencelli there are slight earthwork remains of a medieval castle, but the unexpectedly large church of St Meugan with its fifteenth-century tower and waggon-roof nave is half a mile away on the slopes of the mountain. In the church-yard there are graves of a bride and groom and their friends, all of whom were unfortunately drowned while crossing the Usk in 1753 on their way to the marriage service.

Llanfrynach is a quiet village, closely knit around a rebuilt church and a large churchyard, a mile further on. The un-Welsh layout of the village is compensated for by a monumental slab (1616) in the church listing in typically Welsh fashion the pedigree of Thomas ap John ap Thomas ap John ap Rosser ap John ap Ieuan ap Philip ap Howell Gam. Behind the village is the site of a bathhouse belonging to a Roman villa. When it was discovered in 1783 it was recorded as having mosaic floors but these have long since been covered over or lost.

Just before joining the main road the way goes near an aqueduct at Brynich and passes close to Aber Cynrig, a small two-storeyed mansion with hipped roofs. Inside there is a moulded ceiling beam dated 1582 but most of the building was refurbished at the end of the seventeenth century. The house is unusual in that it has retained intact a pair of early eighteenth-century paintings (with scenes from the legend of Diana and Actaeon) above the two fireplaces in the hall. John Lloyd, the poet, was born here in 1797 and is chiefly remembered for his long and not very profound narrative poem entitled *The English Country Gentlemen* written in 1849.

Few towns anywhere in Britain are so beautifully situated as Brecon, standing as it does on the gently rising north bank of the graceful Usk, where the fast-running Afon Honddu (after which the town gets its Welsh name, Aberhonddu) has its confluence. Across the Usk are the Brecon Beacons, not so near as to be overwhelming but not too far away for the magnificent outline of their peaks to be lost. As with many old towns Brecon itself, however, is inward

looking and for views of the mountains one must go beyond the
medieval core down to the riverside or up to the modern outskirts
on the hills behind the town.

Much of Brecon's distinctive charm is due to its irregular layout
of narrow medieval streets developing from a triangular market
place in the centre of the town. On one side of this open space is the
parish church of St Mary. Its 100-foot-high tower, built by the
Duke of Buckingham, dates from the sixteenth century. Though
few medieval buildings now remain, the street layout belongs to the
walled borough established by the Normans in 1093. Fragments of
the old town walls and a tower still survive alongside the Captain's
Walk, a promenade built during the Napoleonic wars by French
prisoners. Rather more of the castle sited on the west bank of the
Honddu has managed to withstand the ravages of time and
weather. Originally built by Bernard de Newmarche, the
half-brother of William the Conqueror, the castle now consists of
the thirteenth-century Ely Tower (named after the Bishop of Ely
who was imprisoned here by Richard III) in the grounds of the
Bishop of Swansea and Brecon's private gardens and, on the
opposite side of the road (in the grounds of the Castle of Brecon
Hotel), a thirteenth-century hall.

Before the Industrial Revolution, Brecon was one of the principal
towns of the south and a fashionable centre of social life. The
numerous Jacobean and Georgian town-houses of the local gentry
are still a notable feature of the older part of the town. There was
also a theatre and it was in Brecon that the great tragic actress
Sarah Siddons was born in 1755 at the Shoulder of Mutton Inn (47
High Street). Contemporary with Mrs Siddons were Theophilus
Jones and Thomas Coke. The former, born in 1759 at 12 Lion
Street, was the author of *A History of the County of Brecknock,* while the
latter, born in 1747, became a missionary of the Wesleyan Church
and was also responsible for the establishment of the Wesleyan
Foreign Mission Committee. The Wesleyan Chapel in Lion Street
was built in 1835 to commemorate Dr Coke. Another native of the
town was Sir John Price, a barrister, Secretary of the Council in
Wales and the Marches and principal ecclesiastical registrar to
Henry VIII of England. He was one of the earliest collectors of

Welsh manuscripts and also published the first printed book in Welsh, *Yn y Lhyvyr hwnn*, in 1546.

Of Brecon's nineteenth-century buildings, the most outstanding is the Shirehall with its stately neo-Greek portico. This is now an excellent county museum and has good examples of Celtic inscribed stones, a dug-out canoe of the Dark Ages and Roman finds, as well as natural history and folk-life exhibits. For military history, there is the Regimental Museum at the Watton Barracks nearby, where there are fine collections of uniforms, weapons and medals of the South Wales Borderers.

Two important religious buildings stand outside the medieval town. On the hill overlooking the Honddu is the Cathedral. It was once the Benedictine priory of St John. Its Tithe Barn and Prior's House (now the Deanery) still stand adjacent to the church and together form the most complete group of medieval ecclesiastical buildings in the Principality. The cruciform church has a massive central tower giving it a fortress-like appearance belying the elegance of its interior and, in particular, the beautiful thirteenth-century choir with its walls filled with deeply recessed lancet windows. St Keynes Chapel, on the north side of the nave, was originally the chapel for corvisors (or shoemakers) and tailors. It still retains its ancient screen with a fine ogee arch and has a recessed tomb of a layman (Bloxham) who is thought to have been the builder of the nave. On the bank between the Cathedral and the Honddu is the start of the delightful Priory Groves, a walk laid out some 150 years ago and now a nature trail.

Rather less of the Dominican friary at Llanfaes (beyond the sixteenth-century arched bridge across the Usk) has survived. It is now incorporated in the nineteenth-century buildings of Christ College, one of Wales' pair of Public Schools. The thirteenth-century choir of the friary church remains and now functions as the college chapel, whilst the nave stands as a roofless shell.

There are further religious connections at Llan-ddew, a mile north-east of Brecon. St David's was once one of the mother, or *clas*, churches of Wales and is one of the oldest still standing in Powys. It is massively built, with tiny windows and a tower that has its piers inside the transept crossing. On the opposite side of the road a single arch stands as the sole reminder of a bishop's palace which once stood there. For a few years, at the end of the twelfth century, it was the home of Gerald de Barri (Giraldus Cambrensis) when he occupied the position of Archdeacon of Brecon, which was then an outpost of the far-flung diocese of St David's in Dyfed.

A short walk to the north-west of Brecon brings one to Pen-y-Crug, an Iron-Age hill-fort. The triple line of ramparts and ditches which once defended it is still well preserved and the summit of this bracken covered hill commands a superb panoramic view southwards over the town and across the Vale of Usk towards the Brecon Beacons, the Black Mountains, Fforest Fawr and Y Mynydd Du. Northwards, there are views across Mynydd Epynt. A mile and a half further west at Aberysgir is Y Gaer, the largest Roman auxiliary fort in Wales. Originally built of timber in the first century to house the Spanish Vettonian Cavalry it was partly rebuilt in stone about the middle of the second century. It was re-occupied in the third century and finally abandoned in the latter part of the fourth century. Sir Mortimer Wheeler excavated the fort in 1924 and parts of it, including the foundations of three gateways, a portion of the wall and the corner towers have been left exposed.

The easiest way to the Brecon Beacons from Brecon is by road to Storey Arms (originally a hostelry but now an outdoor activities school) situated at the top of the pass at 1,440 feet above sea level. From Storey Arms there is an easy two-mile walk to Pen-y-fan which at 2,906 feet above sea level is the highest peak south of Cadair Idris in Gwynedd. A far more interesting circular route is from Cantref (three miles south of Brecon), and then up the Bryn-teg ridge to Cribyn (2,608 feet), and Pen-y-fan; the way back is over the shoulder of Carn Du (2,863 feet) and down to lovely Llyn Cwmllwch (a small tarn with a legendary island), past some waterfalls and into the pretty Ffrwdgrech valley. In fine weather, the Beacons make superb hill-walking country with glorious views all around (south across the Severn Sea to Exmoor and north to Pumlumon and even on occasions, as far as Cadair Idris, 60 miles away), but in misty weather the northern escarpments, etched by glaciers of the Ice Age into almost precipitous cliffs, can be as dangerous for the unwary as the cliffs of Snowdonia. To emphasise the point there is a stone monument near Carn Du commemorating the death of little five-year-old Tommy Jones who got lost when out walking on his own.

To the west of the Beacons is Fforest Fawr (Great Forest), a barren undulating moorland area dissected by parallel rivers flowing south towards Swansea Bay. Originally a royal hunting forest, it was farmed out after the Middle Ages, but remained Crown Land until the early nineteenth century. North of Fan Fawr (2,509 feet), the highest peak of the Fforest, is Craig Cerig-gleisiad, an armchair-shaped *cwm* formed by glacial erosion. It is now a National Nature Reserve and here an arctic tundra type of vegetation (a relic of the last great Ice Age), which includes Cowberry, Green Spleenwart and Purple Saxifrage, has survived on the craggy cliffs as well as the more temperate Welsh poppy. Here also is the home of the Buzzard.

The more friendly common of Mynydd Illtud lies further north. Amongst the heathland and marshy pools is the mountain centre, a purpose-built building opened in 1966, providing a lounge, viewing terraces, picnic areas and car park, as well as information on all aspects of the Brecon Beacons National Park. Llanilltud church nearby is nineteenth century and of no particular interest, but the circular *llan* (churchyard) surrounding the church dates from the Dark Ages and in May and June is a colourful carpet of bluebells. Sarn Helen, one of the Roman roads that crosses mid-Wales from north to south, and a Bronze Age *cromlech* (Bedd Illtud) add an air of mystery to the place while not far away are the ruins of Castell Cwmcamlais (or Maescar Castle as it is otherwise known), a reminder of one of the Welsh wars of independence. The castle, probably built by Llewelyn II and destroyed by Edward I, now comprises the stump of a large thirteenth-century stone tower surrounded by a deep dry-moat.

South of Fforest Fawr the scenery changes dramatically from open moorland to deep, narrow and densely wooded valleys. As the rivers that water these valleys come down from Fforest Fawr, on their way to the sea, they cross from the Old Red Sandstone rocks to Carboniferous Limestone rocks giving rise in the process to numerous waterfalls, underground rivers and caves. The area is of exceptional scenic and geological interest but requires time to explore and can only really be seen on foot. The little village of Ystradfellte is a good centre to start from.

The first place of interest is Porth-yr-ogof (Gateway of the Cave) where the Mellte, after running underground for some distance, reappears briefly only to disappear again into a vast cavern. The cave with its maze of side passages can be entered in dry weather for some distance without equipment except a light, but in flood conditions this is impossible. The river reappears from the cave about a quarter of a mile further on. There are many other caves near Ystradfellte and at Pwll-y-rhyd on the Afon Nedd, including one with five miles of underground passages, but these are all potentially dangerous and are for experts only.

Below Porth-yr-ogof a footpath leads in about a mile to the first of the three Clun-gwyn waterfalls. Of the three falls the most beautiful is the middle Clun-gwyn with its single leap followed immediately by a tumbling cascade. The footpath continues through the woods well above the Mellte river to a tributary, the Afon Hepste. Here there are two splendid falls. The lower one is a rapid and like most of the other falls in the district is best seen after wet weather. A short way further up the Hepste is Scwd-yr-Eira, a well-named fall meaning the 'spout of snow'. This is perhaps the best of all the falls and is unusual in that one can walk (with care) behind the 50-foot curtain of water as it drops in a graceful curve over the ledge above. Below the confluence of the Mellte and Hepste the way, though exquisitely beautiful, is extremely difficult because of the steepness of the ravine's sides, which here is a 200- to 300-foot deep gorge.

To explore the valleys west of Ystradfellte take the road along the ridge southwards to Pontneddfechan (Pontneath Vaughan) and join the footpath alongside the Afon Nedd. About a mile upstream the Nedd is joined by the Afon Pyrddin with its two beautiful waterfalls. Scwd Gwladys, the nearer of the two falls, is graceful and easily accessible, while Scwd Einon-gam is perhaps more spectacular but difficult to approach except along the bed of the river when it is dry. After crossing over the Pyrddin by a footbridge continue a mile up the west bank of the Nedd to Pont Melin-fach passing on the way two cataracts and two fine falls known as Scwd Ddwli Isaf and Scwd Ddwli Uchaf. At Pont-Melin-Fach one can continue upstream for a further two and a half miles to Pwll-y-Rhyd where the river disappears underground for a short distance or, alternatively, take to the road again and continue to Ystradfellte.

From Ystradfellte a mountin road follows the line of the Roman road, Sarn Helen, northwards again to the Usk valley. Near the highest point, it passes Maen Llia, an isolated Early Christian memorial stone, and then zig-zags down a steep escarpment into the Senni valley leading eventually to the upper part of the Usk valley at Sennybridge.

Sennybridge was largely developed in the early nineteenth century when, after the opening of the turnpike road, it took over the sheep and cattle market which had originally been held in nearby Defynnog. The Sennybridge sheep sales were started by Scottish farmers who bought large areas of sheep-walks after the enclosure of Fforest Fawr in 1815-19. On the opposite side of the river there is an army camp serving the Mynydd Epynt artillery range.

Betws Pen-pont lies a short way east of Sennybridge in a delightful situation along a fine stretch of the Usk. There is an unusual church and two large mansions but no village. Between them they form a fascinating group of buildings. The earliest of the two mansions is Pen-pont, which was built in the late seventeenth century by Daniel Williams with money acquired by successive marriages to two rich heiresses. The classical colonnade in front of the house was added in 1815. Nearby is a small dower house, with a richly carved pediment, built for Daniel Williams' son. The unusual church at Betws Pen-pont has a circular tower and steeple and a semi-circular east end. It is the result of rebuilding in 1865 by Sir Gilbert Scott. Abercamlais, the other mansion in this group, was built probably in the early eighteenth century by another branch of the Williams family. Both houses still retain their dovecotes. Pen-pont's is plain and square, but the two-storey octagonal dovecot at Abercamlais is more ornamental and also has a multi-purpose use – the upper part is for the doves while the lower part serves as a privy and also forms a bridge across the stream.

A couple of miles west of Sennybridge is Trecastell. The large motte-and-bailey castle which towers above the road was built by the Lord of Brecknock in the twelfth century to guard the valley from the west. A mile further on is Llywel church with its tall fifteenth-century tower, churchyard stocks and inside a colony of Natterer's bats and two Early Christian stones with Ogham (Irish) inscriptions.

The last major mountain in the chain of mountains that stretches from east to west across the Brecon Beacons National Park is Y Mynydd Du (otherwise known as the Black Mountain– a needless Anglicisation that only results in confusion with the Black Mountains at the eastern end of the Park). It forms the boundary between two counties (Powys and Dyfed) and has two peaks (Bannau Brycheiniog, 2,632 feet, and Bannau Sir Gaer, 2,460 feet), which look down precipitously on to two lakes (Llyn y Fan Fawr and Llyn y Fan Fach), 700 feet below.

Emerging from the northern slopes of Y Mynydd Du are the sources of two important rivers, the Usk (or as it is known here, Afon Wysg) and the Tawe. For the first few miles the Usk stream goes steadily north, passing a number of small Bronze-Age stone circles each accompanied by an avenue of small stones and all largely hidden now by undergrowth, and then after passing through the very attractive Cwmwysg reservoir it turns suddenly eastwards on its journey, now as a fully fledged river, towards Sennybridge and Brecon.

The Tawe, on the other hand, starts by going east and then makes a sharp turn south following a course below the long, dark escarpment of Fan Hir. At Glyntawe the river crosses a narrow band of limestone and the scenery changes once again from open moorland to a deep, winding and well-wooded valley with rocky outcrops. Here within the short space of half-a-mile are two places of unusual interest, one natural and the other man-made.

The natural feature is Dan-yr-ogof, a marvellous cave system which is illuminated and open to the public. The caves were first discovered and explored in 1912 by two local brothers, Ashwell and Jeff Morgan, who found a chain of underground lakes, natural bridges and an underground waterfall as well as some fine stalactites and stalagmites. For 25 years no more was heard of the caves and then in 1938 they were re-explored by properly trained cavers and a year later opened to the public. The guided tour of just over a mile lasts about 45 minutes. In 1971 an adjoining cave known as the cathedral cave, because of its vast 80-foot-high cavern, was also opened to the public. Ogof Ffynnon Ddu, the largest cave in Wales with 16 miles of caverns and passages, is also situated in the Tawe valley amongst the Carreg-lwyd quarries.

The man-made curiosity of this romantic valley is Craig-y-Nos (Rock of the Night), a Gothic castle first built about 1840 and later extended with Italianate additions. It is now a hospital but for 40 years it was the home and refuge of Adelina Patti, the Victorian *prima donna*, who returned here by special train after each triumphant tour of the world's opera houses; at the station she had her own private waiting room. Born in Madrid of Italian parents and brought up in New York, Madame Patti was 36 when she came to Wales and bought Craig-y-Nos, but by then she was well on the way to amassing one of the largest fortunes ever made by an opera singer. Her first marriage, however, to the Marquis de Chaux, was not a success, and in 1885 they were divorced. A year later Madame Patti married the tenor Ernesto Nicolini and together they set about transforming Craig-y-Nos. Wings were added on, a clock tower built, a beautiful conservatory (later re-erected at Swansea) with tropical plants was constructed, a private theatre opened and, in addition to all this, a suite of rooms was prepared and set apart for the use of the Prince of Wales – later King Edward VII. The delightful little theatre is still intact and is now used by local opera groups. In 1898 Nicolini died and Patti married again, this time Baron Cederstrom, who was 26 years her junior. Adelina Patti died in 1919 and left Craig-y-Nos for the last time to be taken to Paris and buried in Père Lachaise Cemetery.

A couple of miles downstream the Tawe turns southwest and, as industry takes over from the rural landscape at Aber-craf and Ystradgynlais, the valley becomes known as the Swansea Valley and Powys and the National Park are left behind.

CHAPTER SIX

Swansea And
The Glamorgan Coast

Swansea, lying at the mouth of the Tawe river and hence known in Welsh as Abertawe, is the second city of Wales and is to Cardiff what Glasgow is to Edinburgh. While Cardiff in the nineteenth century was merely an exporting centre for iron and coal and is now largely concerned with administrative affairs, Swansea was once the metallurgical capital of the world and is still busily industrial. Cardiff dates back to Roman times but Swansea seems to have been nothing before the coming of the Normans, though its name (meaning Sweyn's Island), may in fact be of Viking origin. Even in the layout of its streets Swansea, despite post-war replanning of the centre, appears formless compared with the rigid 'T' junction of Cardiff's main shopping streets and the formality of Cathays Park. Outside the commercial centre of Swansea the terraces come tumbling down the hillside as though some of the terraces of the mining valleys had escaped and sought refuge here within sight of the sea. Indeed, there is much of the spirit and humanity of the Valleys here for while Cardiff, like Edinburgh, is aloof, Swansea is warm like Glasgow and thoroughly Welsh in spirit if not in language.

Swansea's oldest building is the castle in the centre of the city. The remains that can be seen now are those of a fortified manor house built in the early fourteenth century by Bishop Henry de Gower and embellished with a splendid arcaded parapet similar to the parapets which ornament Gower's other palaces at St David's and Lamphey. In the early fifteenth century the mansion was largely destroyed by Owain Glyndŵr just two centuries earlier the first stone castle on the site had been destroyed by Llewelyn I in his attempt to unite Wales.

Swansea suffered heavily from enemy action during the Second World War and much of the centre, including the main shopping area, has since been completely rebuilt. One of the victims of the destruction and reconstruction was the home of the remarkable Beau Nash. He was born in College Street in 1674 and after schooling in Carmarthen went to seek his fortune at Bath where, after establishing himself as master of ceremonies and the undisputed dictator of manners he developed Bath into a leading centre of fashion.

Princess Way crosses the shopping centre at right-angles and leads towards the docks. Halfway along it is St Mary's Church, another victim of the Second World War and since restored. At the docks end of Princess Way, and set apart from the rest of the town centre, the stately Royal Institution of South Wales in York Street looks forlorn and lost. It is one of Swansea's three museums. Behind its grand Ionic portico are exhibitions dealing with the archaeology, natural history and industrial history of the locality. There are also relics of the old Mumbles Railway (actually a four-mile-long tramcar line that ran along the edge of the sands), and souvenirs of Edgar Evans, one of Scott's companions on his journey to the South Pole. The Maritime Museum, behind the Royal Institution, is housed in a former dock warehouse and includes both industrial and transport exhibits as well as those to do with the sea.

The other museum, the Glynn Vivian Art Gallery in Alexandra Road to the north of the town centre, has fine collections of paintings and of British and Continental china and glass. Its most prized exhibits are fine examples of the porcelain for which Swansea is justly famous. Swansea porcelain is comparatively rare for it was only made for a few brief years early in the nineteenth century. Long before that china had been made at the Cambrian Pottery in Swansea, but it was not until Lewis Weston Dillwyn took over the works in 1814 that porcelain was produced in Swansea. The beautifully decorated work produced during this period is comparable with the best porcelain made in Europe, but unfortunately the softpaste had certain peculiarities as a result of which it was more than usually difficult to manufacture successfully. In 1824 the pottery reverted to production of earthenware and finally closed in 1870.

The metal· industries were the greatest boost to Swansea's development in the nineteenth century. The first of these industries was copper smelting, which started in the early eighteenth century when Cornish ore was brought to the little seaside town. By the middle of the nineteenth century more than half of the copper works in Britain were sited in Swansea or within a few miles of the prospering town. Copper smelting, however, was but one of the industries that helped the Swansea district to become recognised as a great metallurgical metropolis. Other notable local industries were the smelting of lead and silver ores, cobalt, gold and nickel. By the end of the nineteenth century Swansea was also the main centre in Britain for both zinc and tin-plate.

Some of the largest and most important of these manufactories were situated at Morriston, four miles to the north. It was here, in 1768, that one of the earliest experiments in town planning was carried out by Sir John Morris in order to attract and house labour for his copper works. He employed William Edwards, the bridge-builder of Pontypridd, to design the layout to a gridiron plan. Streets were laid out on spacious lines and at the centre a church was built on an island at the crossing of the two main streets. Although most of the buildings have long since been rebuilt the layout remains the same. The island church still stands but has been reduced in visible significance by the building of Tabernacl Chapel nearby in 1873. Referred to, sometimes, as 'the great Cathedral of Welsh Nonconformity' Tabernacl is, with its soaring spire and its arcaded front, one of the most striking of all Welsh chapels in appearance. It is also the home of one of Wales' best-known choirs.

Swansea is a city of contrasts, where industry and tourism compete and manage to survive almost side by side. As a seaside resort its great attraction is the miles of safe, sandy beaches that fringe the beautiful curving coastline of Swansea Bay ending on the western side in a rocky peninsula at Mumbles Head. The eastern

side of the bay near Port Talbot has now succumbed to industry but even this is subdued by the mountainous background and the overall view of the bay is still very fine. The poet Walter Savage Landor compared it to the Bay of Naples when he wrote to a friend from Italy that 'the Gulf of Salerno is much finer than Naples, but give me Swansea for scenery and climate'.

Another lover of Swansea Bay was Ann Julia Kemble, the sister of the actress Sarah Siddons. She was known as 'Ann of Swansea' and came to live in the town in 1799. Although a prolific novelist and poetess, little of her work is now remembered or has even survived. Her 50 volumes of novels have been almost entirely forgotten and of her poems only the sorrowful 'Swansea Bay' is generally known.

Overlooking the Bay, about a mile from the town centre is the Guildhall, an imposing building in smooth neo-Classical style with a tall rectangular clocktower. It was erected in 1934 to the designs of Sir Percy Thomas. The main hall is known as the Brangwyn Hall and houses 16 great mural panels by Sir Frank Brangwyn. The panels were designed to illustrate the natural and human wealth of the British Empire and were originally intended to hang in the Royal Gallery of the House of Lords in London. The Fine Arts Commission, however, found them to be too controversial for such an elevated place. Fortunately for Wales, Swansea offered to take then instead. They now form a fine background to the Swansea Festival of Music and the Arts which is held here every year, in October.

The road from Swansea to Oystermouth and the Mumbles hugs the curving coast of Swansea Bay for five miles before petering out on the rocky Mumbles Head. Bordering the road just after leaving Swansea is the university campus in the grounds of Singleton Park. The University College of Swansea was established in 1920 and most of the departments are now housed in a varied assortment of modern buildings. Part of the college, however, still uses Singleton Abbey, a Tudor-style mansion built in 1826 for Lord Swansea (John Henry Vivian) with 13 staircases but only one bath.

At Oystermouth there is a fine castle delightfully situated in a hillside park. The earliest remains, those of the keep, are mid-thirteenth century, but the best part is the early fourteenth-century chapel tower with its delicate traceried windows.

Oystermouth's later claim to fame was as the home of Thomas Bowdler, the self-appointed censor of Shakespeare. Although Bowdler was a fervent admirer of Shakespeare he nevertheless believed that a great deal of the playwright's work was unfit to be heard in public. He therefore went through all the plays with his blue pencil and eventually brought out a ten-volume *Family Shakespeare* in which all 'words and expressions which are of such a nature as to raise a blush on the cheek of modesty' were omitted. Bowdler died in 1825 and was buried in the graveyard of Oystermouth Church. There is a monument to Dr Bowdler in the churchyard, but perhaps his most permanent memorial is the word 'bowdlerize', meaning 'to expurgate', now found in every English dictionary.

The Mumbles is the name used for the little peninsula jutting out into Swansea Bay and forming the south-eastern corner of Gower. At Mumbles Head there is a pier and lifeboat station and beyond that a couple of rocky islets, the farthest of which has a lighthouse dating from 1784.

Gower is the large peninsula lying between Swansea Bay and Carmarthen Bay. Because of its superb coastal scenery most of the peninsula has been declared an Area of Outstanding Natural Beauty. As one goes west from the Mumbles the coast and countryside become progressively wilder and the views more dramatic. For 16 miles, from Mumbles Head to Worm's Head, there is an almost continuous line of rugged cliffs, interspersed here and there with sandy coves and thickly wooded cwms.

The first two coves at Langland Bay and Caswell Bay, are backed by holiday and residential development that are really extensions of Oystermouth. Next, there is the unspoilt Pwll-du Bay where the narrow and winding gorge of the Bishopston valley opens on to the sea. This is limestone country and the stream which feeds the valley goes underground for some distance before emerging from a cave about a mile inland. To the west of Pwll-du Bay are two sea caves where palaeolithic bones have been found. In one of these,

Bacon Hole, there are also some red ochre marks which were once believed to have been remnants of some prehistoric cave painting but are now thought to be of natural origin. At Minchin Hole pieces of pottery have been found along with the bones of mammoth and rhinoceros.

Three Cliffs Bay, further west, gets its name from three jagged cliffs that project out from the mainland and protect the sandy beach where Pennard Pill enters the sea. The eastern side of the Pennard valley is largely covered by blown sand dunes. By the sixteenth century the sand had reached as far as Pennard Castle and was encroaching on the church. Both buildings were abandoned soon after and although now the castle stands as an impressive ruin the old church, like that of Penmaen on the opposite side of the valley, has largely disappeared from sight, under the dunes. Further inland, at Parkmill, there is a good example of a prehistoric burial chamber (known as Parc le Breos) in the midst of the woods that here fill the valley on both sides.

Beyond Three Cliffs Bay the coast curves southwards in a wide sweep past Oxwich Burrows (a National Nature Reserve), to a bulky headland at Oxwich Point. The little village of Oxwich lies in the lee of the headland and overlooks the nature reserve where the mouth of the river has been blocked by wind-blown sand dunes to form an extensive marsh incorporating a number of freshwater pools. Oxwich Castle looks at first like a large straggling farm, but is really a sixteenth-century mansion built on the site of a medieval fortress. The main part of the mansion is in ruins and the enormous hall which once covered the whole of the first floor is now open to the sky. It was built by the Mansel family when they abandoned Penrice Castle a mile or so to the north.

Port Eynon, a couple of miles further along the coast, has a narrow tortuous street descending steeply to a fine sandy beach. By the churchyard there is a life-like memorial to the lifeboat crew drowned in 1916 while out rescuing a ship in distress. After this disaster the local lifeboat service was discontinued in favour of more modern lifeboats from the Mumbles and Tenby. The lifeboat house is now a youth hostel. Below the village is Culver Hole, a natural cave artificially closed by a masonry wall with circular and rectangular windows. According to local legend it was a smugglers' den, for being so isolated this part of the coast was a favourite haunt for smugglers, but it may have originally been a columbarium.

After Port Eynon the cliffs become continuous and more precipitous. Along the top of the cliffs, there is an excellent five-mile cliff walk to Rhosili. Below are the Paviland Caves, famous in archaeological circles for the discovery in 1823 of a prehistoric skeleton in one of the caves. The bones had been dyed red by iron oxide and the skeleton became known as the Red Lady of Paviland. Later examination showed that the bones were, in fact, the remains of a man of the Old Stone Age period.

Rhosili, the remotest of the Gower villages, is a small collection of cottages and an old gable-towered church set at the edge of the plateau overlooking the sea at the farthest corner of the peninsula. On the north wall of the church there is a plaque to Petty Officer Edgar Evans who died with Scott on their return trip from the South Pole. The only road hereabouts is that into the village, so that any exploration has to be done on foot. The district is full of interest, however, and it is worth spending some time exploring it. From Rhosili one can see, off the south-west headland, the serpent-like island known as Worm's Head. The name Worm is of Viking origin and means dragon. The mile-long island has two rocky heads connected by a thin, curving neck called the Devil's Bridge. For most of the time it is a true island completely surrounded by water, but for a couple of hours on either side of low-water it becomes a peninsula accessible (with care) across a rocky causeway. Above the cliffs between Rhosili and Worm's Head is an area known as the 'Vile', or 'Viel', where there is a remarkable survival of an ancient open-field system still with its long, narrow strip fields unchanged since the Middle Ages.

North of Rhosili there is a splendid sandy beach backed by the long, steep ridge of Rhosili Down (632 feet), the highest point in Gower. On the ridge there are numerous prehistoric remains including two ruined burial chambers known as Sweyne's Howes. Rhosili beach is 250 feet below the village and is only accessible at the southern end by a winding footpath. The golden beach extends northwards for three miles in a gentle curve past Llangennith and then merges into huge sand dunes that extend for another four miles to Whitford Burrows on the north coast of Gower.

The distance on foot between Rhosili and Llangennith is a mere two and a quarter miles. By road, (mainly along narrow winding lanes), the distance is nine miles! Llangennith itself is comparatively open, with houses scattered around a green, and lies in a bowl between Rhosili Down and Llanmadoc Hill. Off the coast at Llangennith Burrows is the little island of Burry Holm, with remains of a promontory fort and a number of ecclesiastical settlements. The earliest ecclesiastical remains excavated may well have been the chapel attributed to the sixth-century St Cenydd after whom Llangennith was named. A tiny twelfth-century church and outbuildings on the island probably formed the dependent cell of the mainland priory and seems to have been the home for a while of a prior who caused a scandal during the time of Giraldus Cambrensis by carrying on an adulterous affair with a local girl. The prior was given a warning and promised to mend his ways, but he soon renewed his association and began living openly with the girl until the bishop was informed whereupon he was dismissed. Later still, a new church was built in the fourteenth century alongside a substantial hall-house.

The north coast of Gower changes dramatically after Whitford Burrows. There is still a line of cliffs on this side of the peninsula, but they are some way inland – the sea here having become silted up – and are muted in comparison with rocky sea cliffs of the southern coast. Weobly Castle (a strongly fortified mansion of the fourteenth century) stands on the top of the old cliff line and overlooks a vast area of marshes, saltings and treacherous sands on the shore of the Loughor estuary. Beyond the estuary are the industrial chimneys of Llanelli, in Dyfed.

Two roads lead back to Swansea. The northern one continues alongside the estuary as far as Penclawdd (famous for its cockle industry) and then on through the industrial belt. The more southerly route crosses the coastal heathlands of Gower and passes close to Swansea Airport before entering Swansea at the upper end of the thickly wooded Clyne valley.

East of Swansea the narrow coastal plain has become heavily

industrialised as far as Margam. At Neath, the main urban centre of the area, industry extends a few miles inland along the once unspoilt Vale of Neath. Neath itself, although since the early eighteenth century a centre for copper smelting and other metal industries, has a history going back almost two thousand years. Beneath one of its newer housing estates, for instance, there are remains of the Roman fort of Nidum. There is also a twelfth-century parish church, scant remains of a castle and the more extensive remains of a Benedictine abbey, forlorn now and blackened by industrial smoke. More surprising, perhaps, to the visitor are the Bird Gardens on the hillside grounds of Penscynor House at Cilfrew, just north of Neath. Curiously, Penscynor House was built (1856) for Thomas Leyson, a direct descendant of the last abbot of Neath Abbey, also Thomas Leyson. There is a wide variety of birds from all parts of the world as well as numerous smaller animals in the Gardens, but pride of place goes to the Tropical House where one can see exotic humming birds darting hither and thither and feeding and washing at a miniature waterfall.

North-east of Neath the perfectly shaped Vale of Neath becomes less and less industrialised and even where isolated pockets of industry occur they are often shielded and partially enclosed by woodlands. At Melin-cwrt, where a tributary stream crosses the steep sides of the Vale, there is a splendid 80-foot-high waterfall.

The extensive woodlands on both sides of the Vale of Neath are part of Coed Morgannwg, an enormous forest, which, with an area of 55 square miles is the largest in Wales. The forest extends southwards to Margam across mountainous country sharply dissected by narrow, winding valleys. Most of the valleys contain small mining villages, but their industrial character is completely transformed by the dominating loveliness of the afforested hillsides. A large part of the deep Afan valley and its tributary valley, Cwm yr Argoed, in the middle of the forest has now been developed into an excellent country park.

The Afan valley emerges into the restricted coastal plain at Port Talbot, a fast-growing industrial and seaside town, which has now expanded to take in both Margam and Aberafan. Taken together the three places are an unusual mixture of contrasting communities wedged between mountain and sea. Port Talbot itself has both the largest purpose-made deep-water harbour and the largest steel strip-mill in Britain. At Aberafan, north-west of the harbour, there is a modern lido and entertainment centre, a large amusement park and fun-fair and a two-mile expanse of sandy beach. Marga, to the south-east, contents itself with history and architecture centered on a half-ruined abbey in a romantic setting by the side of a lake. Margam Abbey, founded by the Cistercians in 1147, is only half-ruined because the nave is still used as a parish church. In the ruined, privately owned half of the abbey there is a beautiful twelve-sided chapter house and over the buried foundations of the domestic quarters, there is an exceptionally long orangery, built in 1787 to protect orange and lemon trees from the winter frost. According to popular tradition the trees were part of a present sent by sea from Portugal to the king but the vessel was shipwrecked on the neighbouring coast and its cargo claimed by the lord of the manor.

Margam Abbey is also the name for the early-nineteenth century mansion near the church. Dominated by a great octagonal tower in the centre, the mansion is a vigorous mixture of pinnacles, chimneys, gables, crenellated parapets, buttresses and varied windows, all designed to give the impression of the accumulation of centuries of construction. More architecturally elegant is the octagonal-shaped nonconformist chapel built about the same time at Margam Groes.

The hills and mountains immediately behind Margam are littered with the remains of ancient hill-forts, camps, earthworks and burial mounds of past civilisations. The area was also a rich hunting ground for memorial stones and Celtic crosses, but most of these have now been collected together and are on view at the Margam Stones Museum in the old schoolhouse near Margam Abbey.

From Margam the secondary road to Porth-cawl follows the line of a Roman road known variously as Via Julia Maritima, Heol y Sheet and Water Street. Just beyond the main railway line the road crosses the tip of a sandy desert that in the sixteenth century overwhelmed and destroyed the Norman borough of Kenfig. The borough of Kenfig and its corporation were not, incidentally, abolished until 1883, some three centuries later: until then the borough, along with other Glamorgan boroughs, still returned members to parliament. All that is now visible are some bare ruins of Kenfig Castle. The rest of the town, including the church and town walls, lies buried under the sand, waiting for some future archaeologist to uncover its secrets. The inundation appears to have started gradually, but by the fourteenth century the advancing sands were troublesome enough for warning to be issued against any act likely to make encroachment easier, and by 1540 when Leland visited the site the town was 'in ruins and almost shokid an devourid with the sandes that the Severn Se ther castith up'. Surprisingly, the mysterious freshwater lake to the south, known as Kenfig Pool, although surrounded by sand, never became blocked up.

A mile south of Kenfig Pool is Sker House, the setting for the once popular *The Maid of Sker*, by R. D. Blackmore, the author of *Lorna Doone*. At Sker Point the sandy beach gives way briefly to rocks while the sand dunes change to low cliffs which continue on past the Royal Porthcawl Golf Club to Porth-cawl itself.

Porth-cawl, now a breezy and popular seaside resort, was a small port of some antiquity before it was suddenly brought into prominence in the mid-nineteenth century as an outlet for the limestone, coal and iron ore of the hills to the north. A railway was built and a quay and dock constructed, but in the face of competition from better-placed ports it never achieved the great hopes held for it and now the dock has been filled in to make a car park. The little harbour and quay at the end of the Esplanade still remain, however, and add interest to the town. East of the harbour there are two fine beaches, Sandy Bay and Trecco Bay, and behind these, where once were sand dunes, there is a giant fun-fair called Coney Beach, and an immense caravan park for 3,000 caravans.

Further east is Merthyr Mawr Warren, another vast wilderness of lonely grass-covered sand dunes (some rising to 200 feet) that continue on irresistibly until the Ogwr (Ogmore) river brings them all to a sudden stop. Occasionally, after the sands have been blown about, various ancient implements and brooches come to the surface and these, together with excavations, have shown that the site was occupied in the New Stone Age, the Bronze Age and the Early Iron Age. In odd places walls and corners of later buildings still protrude through the dunes, while at the north-eastern edge of the warren there are the ruins of Candleston Castle, a fifteenth-century fortified mansion.

The picturesque village of Merthyr Mawr is another echo from the past. Casually placed cottages with thatched roofs exude an air of peace and contentment and nothing seems to have changed since its little church of St Teilo was rebuilt in 1848. In the grounds of Merthyr Mawr House there are the ruins of St Roques Chapel, a small oratory placed on top of an ancient hill-fort, where a number of Celtic crosses found in the locality have been collected together.

Traditionally the lowland area between the Ogwr in the west and the Taf in the east is known as the Vale of Glamorgan, or in Welsh Bro Morgannwg, to distinguish it from the valleys and mountains (Blaenau Morgannwg) to the north. It is not in fact a vale but rather a pleasant undulating plateau with many neat, tightly-knit villages. That it was one of the earliest parts to be settled by the Normans can be seen by the unusually high proportion of un-Welsh place names. There are, for instance, as many parish place-names beginning with the word 'Saint' as there are starting with 'Llan'.

To defend their newly-won territories the Norman lords built numerous castles here, as in all other parts of Wales where they had gained a hold. Three of these castles were built in and near Bridgend to form a defensive triangle. Newcastle, standing on a hill above a fifteenth-century hospice and an eighteenth-century bridge at Bridgend, has few remains though it is of interest for the unusually elaborate decoration to its Norman gateway. Coety Castle, the largest and most splendid of the three, lies just east of Bridgend. It was first built by Payn de Turbeville, a Norman marcher lord who is reputed to have won the land without bloodshed by marrying the daughter of Morgan the Welsh ruler of the district. Ogmore Castle (named after the Afon Ogwr but actually on a tributary) guarded an important river crossing between east and west. Although ruined it is in a delightful rural setting and still manages to look picturesque. The stepping stones across the river immediately in front of the castle lead back to Merthyr Mawr half a mile away.

The outstanding building in this district is not a castle but Ewenni Priory just outside Bridgend. Dating from the early twelfth century it has great cylindrical piers, simple round arches and is probably the finest example of an early Norman church in Wales. From the outside the erstwhile monastery has an impressive fortress-like appearance, an impression that is reinforced by the battlemented walls and towers that surround the precinct.The interior is, for a Romanesque building, sparsely decorated but what there is adds to the dignity of this remarkably unspoilt church. Like Margam Abbey the nave of Ewenni Priory is still in use as the parish church.

Llantwit Major, or more correctly Llanilltud Fawr, is famous for a monastery that has virtually disappeared without trace. This is the fifth-century Celtic monastery of St Illtud which was reputed to have had seven halls, 400 houses and 2,000 pupils. In the Dark Ages it became renowned as a centre of learning, attracting students from all over Wales and western England, and it was also a busy mission centre for founding new churches, yet nothing solid remains to show where the monastery was sited or what it looked like. The church, halls and individual cells were probably of timber and this would account for the lack of any remains. Traditionally, the site of the monastery is supposed to be just north of the present church of St Illtud and maybe the ancient foundations still lie buried beneath later houses.

St Illtud's Church is a curious mixture of different periods of building strung out, in line, one behind the other. The Western (or old) Church was the original parish church built on Norman, or perhaps pre-Norman foundations. A tall, slim tower was built onto the eastern end in the thirteenth century and was followed by a new Eastern (or Monastic) Church and chancel while at the the far western end of the original building the Lady Chapel (or Galilee), now in ruins, was added. Inside there are traces of a number of medieval wall paintings and in the Western Church a remarkable collection of memorial stones and carved Celtic crosses that bear moving testimony to the renown of this hallowed centre of Welsh Christianity.

Although Llantwit has grown considerably in recent years, due to its nearness to the Air Force base at St Athan, the winding, narrow and high-walled streets of the town centre still preserve its ancient character. The town also retains a number of fine old buildings, including a fifteenth-century town hall, a medieval gatehouse and circular dovecote near the church and some sixteenth-century inns and houses. A mile to the south, near Col-hugh Beach, there are ditches and earthworks belonging to an Early Iron-Age fort. St Donat's Castle, a couple of miles to the west of Llantwit, is a thirteenth-century fortress which has been lived in continuously since the time it was built. To meet the needs of its inhabitants the castle has continually undergone alteration and extension, most notably in the early part of this century when it was bought by Randolph Hearst, an American newspaper magnate, and completely modernised. The Castle is now the home of Atlantic College, an international sixth-form school.

Another place with a long history is the sleepy little village of Llancarfan, buried deep in the interior of the Vale. It, too, has an ancient fort defended by ditches and in the Dark Ages was associated with the monastic college of another famous Celtic saint, St Cadoc. Apart from a disproportionately large church there is little now to remind one of the village's earlier fame or of some of the notables who lived there. In addition to St Cadoc, there were also Caradoc and Walter de Mapes, two of the earliest of Welsh historians and both products of the monastic college in the twelfth century. Better known than either of them today is Iolo Morgannwg (Edward Williams), who was born in 1747 at Penn-onn. A stonemason by trade, he taught himself to become both poet and historian and then went on to the realms of literary forgery. Out of a patriotic fervour for his home county he fabricated folk tales, genealogies, records and manuscripts relating to early *eisteddfodau* and bardic ceremonies, all to prove that Glamorgan had a richer tradition than any other county. Before his work was discredited some of the ceremonies which he thought up had already been grafted on to the procedures of the National Eisteddfod and still remain an essential part of it. Needless to say, later historians and literary researchers were extremely upset when they found out that they had been fooled and, not knowing what to believe and to discard, they scorned both Iolo and his work.

Cowbridge, the smallest urban district in Wales until local government reorganisation in 1974, was for long the chief market and most important town in the Vale of Glamorgan and was known as the capital of the Vale. It consists of little more than a single tightly packed street, three-quarters of a mile long and now happily by-passed, but still retains on the south side considerable remains of its medieval town walls, two towers and a gateway. Cowbridge Castle has vanished, but the ruins of another medieval fortress still stand at Llanblethian, half a mile to the south. The grammar school, founded in 1608, is one of the most historic in Wales, but the present buildings are mostly mid-nineteenth century. Alongside the school is the parish church with a curious thirteenth-century tower.

Between Cowbridge and Cardiff there are a number of pretty little villages, many still containing thatched houses. St Nicholas is one of the most pleasant although its rural charm is somewhat shattered by the noise of traffic on the main road.

Dyffryn, a mile to the south, has the largest and most exotic gardens in Glamorgan. They were laid out by the landscape gardener Mawson at the beginning of the present century around Dyffryn House, a late nineteenth-century mansion built in the style of a French château. In front of the mansion there are handsome lawns bisected by a lily canal with fountains at one end. Around these lawns are woods and rock gardens and a variety of smaller areas in different styles, including a Roman garden, a rose garden, a pool garden, sunken gardens and a fountain court. On the other side of Dyffryn House there are greenhouses with collections of cacti, ferns and orchids and a large palm house for tropical and sub-tropical plants.

For those interested in really ancient monuments, there are two good examples of Stone Age burial chambers near Dyffryn Gardens. Of St Lythan's *cromlech* only the upright stones and capstone remain, but at Tinkinswood *cromlech* much of the covering mound as well has survived although it is still possible to enter the burial chamber under its enormous 40-ton capstone.

Today the new capital of the Vale and the only place in the district of any size is the port-cum-seaside-resort of Barry. It was developed from almost nothing in the latter part of the nineteenth century when Cardiff was unable to handle alone the ever-growing volume of coal that came down from the Valleys for export. Barry has a zoo and even scant remains of a castle, but its greatest attraction is Barry Island, the venue for hundreds of Sunday School outings and thousands of holiday-makers every year. No longer an island, however, for the construction of nearby docks involved building a causeway from the mainland, it has wide, sandy beaches, a vast pleasure park with a scenic railway and a large holiday camp.

CHAPTER SEVEN

Introduction To
Western Wales

Western Wales comprises the new county of Dyfed which in turn consists of the old counties of Carmarthenshire (Sir Gaerfyrddin), Pembrokeshire (Sir Benfro) and Cardiganshire (Sir Geredigion). The whole area is really one large peninsula jutting out from the rest of Wales between the Severn Sea and the Celtic Sea. Compared with the rest of the principality the scenery of Dyfed is subdued. Most of the peninsula is less than 1,000 feet above sea level and only in the northern and eastern extremities does it become really wild, with mountains rising to over 2,500 feet. But subdued though the landscape is, it is nearly always handsome and where the land has been etched by the action of mountain glaciers and the timeless sea it is magnificent. The supreme example of this, of course, is the Pembrokeshire Coast National Park which covers most of the coast from east of Tenby to Cardigan and includes most of the Milford Haven and Mynydd Preseli.

The county is almost entirely rural. Heavy industry only occurs in the south-eastern corner where the South Wales coalfield intrudes as far west as Llanelli and Kidwelly. Apart from Llanelli the largest towns have less people than a Cardiff suburb and in England most of the other towns would be classed as large villages. But this is Wales and such things must be judged not by lesser standards but by different standards. Most of the towns stand either on the coast or on the two main rivers – the Tywi and the Teifi – that run down from the mountains south-westwards to the sea. The exception is Haverfordwest, which stands in the middle of the old county of Pembrokeshire on the Western Cleddau river.

History and pre-history have left their impact on Dyfed in many ways. Physically, there is the evidence of prehistoric earthworks, *cromlechau* (burial chambers), Celtic stone crosses and medieval castles, all as numerous here as in any part of Britain. In addition there are ruined abbeys, the greatest cathedral in Wales, modest but fine mansions, and many endearing country churches and chapels. The cultural and spiritual effect of history is just as obvious in the continuity of the Welsh language – north of a line between Carmarthen and St David's two-thirds of the people speak Welsh as their mother tongue – and in the strength of religious nonconformity.

Like the rest of Wales Dyfed also formed part of the Roman empire in the early centuries after Christ. Though the Roman occupation was essentially military in character, conditions in the south-west were sufficiently stable for the development of a small civil town alongside the fort at Carmarthen and for mining to be carried out in the interior uplands. As far as is known, there were only two other permanent forts, at Llandovery to control the route from Brecon to the west and near Llanddewibrefi to guard the road from Carmarthen to the north.

The centuries after the Roman withdrawal were of critical importance in the life of Wales. It was in this period, known as the Age of Saints, that Celtic missionaries or 'saints' did so much to establish Christianity on a firm foundation. Despite the setting up of numerous monasteries and churches the emphasis was always on a spiritual church of sublime power rather than on physical monuments. Nevertheless, nearly 200 recorded Early Christian inscribed and sculptured stones reflect the conversion of this part of Wales to Christianity. Dyfed was one of the major missionary areas of Britain and two of the greatest of the missionaries – Dewi Sant (St David), the patron saint of Wales, and St Teilo, his friend – lived and preached here. From Dyfed later saints crossed the sea to Cornwall and Brittany to strengthen Christianity in those areas.

It was during the Age of the Saints, from the fifth to the ninth centuries, that Wales developed politically into a series of kingdoms. The earliest dynasty was founded by Cunedda, a Romano-British prince who migrated from Strathclyde in Scotland to north-western Wales at the beginning of the fifth century. Cunedda's conquests included Ceredigion which was named after Ceredig, one of his eight sons. By the seventh and eighth centuries, Ceredigion had become joined with the ancient province of Ystrad Tywi to form the principality of Seisyllwg, while the land west of Carmarthen and south of Aberteifi formed another principality known as Dyfed.

By the early tenth century both Seisyllwg and the old Dyfed had become united under Hywel Dda to form Deheubarth, one of the four provinces of ancient Wales and equivalent in extent to the modern county of Dyfed plus the Gower peninsula. By his strong government Hywel succeeded in stemming the raids of the marauding Norsemen and brought a period of peace to his kingdom. Later he attempted to bring unity and peace to the whole of Wales by asserting his rule over Gwynedd in the north and Powys in the east. When this had been achieved Hywel is reputed to have embarked on the codification of the customs of various parts of the country into a single Welsh Law. After Hywel's death in about 950 the political unity of Wales was once more broken although under Hywel's grandson Maredudd ab Owain and under Gruffydd ap Llywelyn Deheubarth was for short periods again reunited with the rest of Wales.

The Earl of Shrewsbury was the first Norman to invade Deheubarth. In 1093 he overran Ceredigion and then established the lordship of Pembroke on the south-western tip of the peninsula. Within a year, however, the Welsh princes had regained all their land except for Pembroke Castle. In the early years of the twelfth century, during the reign of Henry I, the Normans again invaded Deheubarth and this time made more permanent conquests, leaving only Cantref Mawr between the Teifi amd Tywi in Welsh hands. To help keep the Welsh in check Henry settled Flemish immigrants around Haverfordwest. On the death of Henry I in 1135 organised attacks were made on the Normans and the Kingdom of Deheubarth was re-established.

Many attempts were made by the Normans to recreate their lordships, but under Rhys ap Gruffydd (1155-97) Deheubarth remained intact and the invaders were left with only slender holds

on the kingdom. After the death of Rhys the power of Deheubarth rapidly declined while that of the Norman lords increased until eventually a balance between the two was reached. Thus for most of the thirteenth century south-western Wales was divided into two parts, one being the southern coastal strip under Norman domination which soon became anglicised in speech and the other being the rump of Deheubarth (Ceredigion and Cantref Mawr) under the Welsh princes. To this day the latter part remains Welsh in language and culture.

In the latter part of the century, the Welsh, incensed at the growing power of the Anglo-Normans, mounted two wars of independence in 1276-7 and 1282-3. In the second war the Welsh under Llywelyn II seized the castles at Carreg Cennen, Llandovery and Llanbadarn and succeeded in reversing the English advance up the Tywi valley at Llandeilo. Then Llywelyn returned to Gwynedd to throw back the invaders in the north. Deprived of their leader the Welsh in west and central Wales began to lose ground until Llywelyn having removed the danger in the north returned southwards to rally his forces. Soon the Welsh were to lose their leader again, this time permanently, when he was ambushed and killed at the Battle of Irfon Bridge in mid-Wales in December 1282. Llywelyn's brother David assumed the leadership, but in the following July he was captured and executed. With David's death the dream of an independent Welsh state almost died. Deheubarth became the property of the English crown and was then divided up to form the counties of Cardigan and Carmarthen.

Never again, apart from a few brief years at the beginning of the fifteenth century during the third war of independence under Owain Glyndŵr, was Deheubarth to be ruled by a Welsh prince. When Henry Tudor, born at Pembroke, defeated Richard III and ascended the throne of England in 1485 as Henry VII it seemed for a time that Welsh patriotism was to be given a new lease of life. Henry Tudor may indeed have had some special feeling towards his country, but his son Henry VIII did not and the result was that when Wales was formally united with England in 1536 the last flicker of independence was extinguished.

A century later the outbreak of the Civil War saw the whole of

•••••• Boundary of National Parks

— — — County Boundary

0   5   10 Miles

0   5   10   16 Kilometres

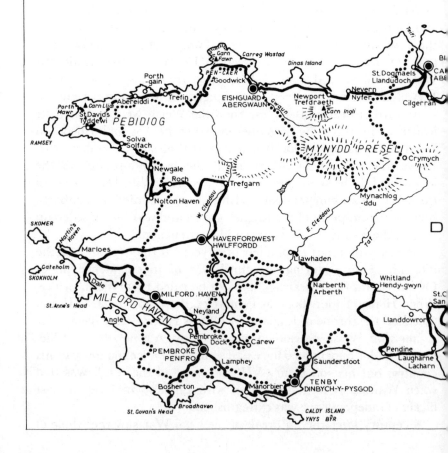

Garn Fawr

Carreg Wastad

Dinas Island

Porth-gain

PEN-CAER

Goodwick

St.Dogmaels
Llandudoch

Abereiddi

Trefin

FISHGUARD
ABERGWAUN

Newport
Trefdraeth

Nevern
Nyfer

Cilgerran

Porth Mawr

Carn Llidi

St Davids
Tyddewi

PEBIDIOG

Gwaun

Carn Ingli

RAMSEY

MYNYDD PRESELI

Solva
Solfach

Crymych

Newgale

Roch

Trefgarn

W. Cleddau

Mynachlog-ddu

Nolton Haven

E. Cleddau

SKOMER

Martin's Haven

Taf

D

Marloes

HAVERFORDWEST
HWLFFORDD

Llawhaden

Gateholm

SKOKHOLM

Dale

Whitland
Hendy-gwyn

St.C
San

MILFORD HAVEN

MILFORD HAVEN

Narberth
Arberth

St.Anne's Head

Neyland

Llanddowror

Angle

Pembroke
Dock

Carew

Pendine

PEMBROKE
PENFRO

Lamphey

Saundersfoot

Laugharne
Lacharn

Bosherton

Manorbier

TENBY
DINBYCH-Y-PYSGOD

St.Govan's Head

Broadhaven

CALDY ISLAND
YNYS BŶR

N

Teifi

BL

CA
ABB

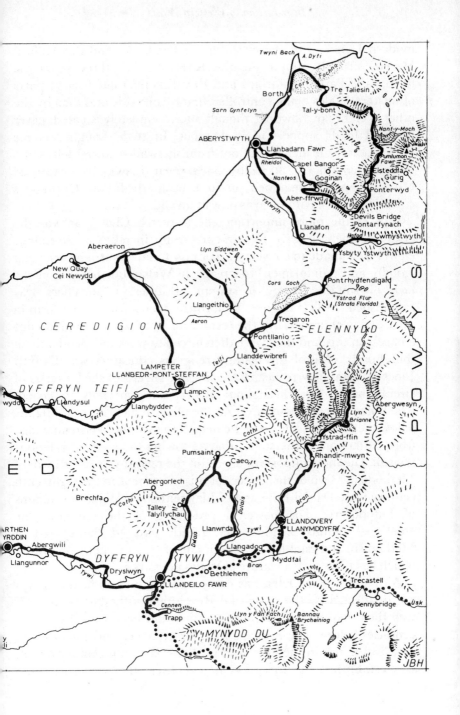

modern Dyfed, with the exception of Pembroke and the Milford Haven, strongly supporting the Royalists. For three years the fortunes of Parliamentarians and Royalists fluctuated: large parts of western Wales being controlled first by one side and then by the other. Pembroke, however, though often completely isolated, never wavered in its support of Parliament. In 1645, Laugharne, the Parliamentary leader, broke out from the walled town, defeated a Royalist contingent at Colby Moor near Llawhaden, captured Carmarthen and marched on to Brecon. As fas as Dyfed was concerned, the Civil War was now at an end.

One of the more important effects of the Civil War was the encouragement it gave to non-conformity in religion. Strenuous efforts were made to convert the country to Puritanism by selecting 'goodly and painful men' to preach in Welsh, but because of the lack of suitable clergy a system of itinerant preachers was established. At first the non-conformists concentrated on reform in the existing churches, but the restoration of royalty in England put a check on this and they were then forced to work independently of the church. One of the leading religious educators was Griffith Jones of Llanddowror near Carmarthen. He established a series of circulating schools throughout Wales, but especially in Dyfed, which had an enormous effect on the life of Wales. By enabling his fellow men to read and write he helped to save the Welsh language from extinction at the same time as sowing the seeds of religious revival. The most important aspect of the revival was the growth of Methodism. Two of the leaders of this movement in the eighteenth century were Daniel Rowland of Llangeitho and William Williams of Llandovery. The powerful preaching of the one and the emotional hymns of the other greatly assisted the spread of Methodism and established the climate of religious non-conformity which has been such a feature of Wales ever since.

Although today Dyfed has comparatively little industry, it was not unaffected by the Industrial Revolution of the last century. It was then a quarry for minerals which had been first discovered centuries before. The Romans had, for instance, worked both gold and lead mines in the hills, and in the seventeenth century a mint was established at Aberystwyth to convert the local silver into coinage. In the nineteenth century mining and quarrying were at their peak. There was coal on the Pembrokeshire coast, slate in the Preseli hills and lead and silver in the mountains of Ceredigion. In addition woollen mills were built where the upland streams debouched on to the larger rivers. Some of these mills, particularly in Duffryn Teifi are still working.

Dyfed is rich too in natural history. Its long coastline, as well as being marvellous scenery, is home for millions of seabirds of all types. The creation of the Pembrokeshire Coast National Park and the establishment of a national nature reserve on the island of Skomer has helped to protect the future of these birds and other coastal wild life. Inland there are also national reserves at Coed Rheidol, Cors Tregaron and Allt Rhyd-y-groes, established mainly for the protection of native plants and trees. They, however, only cover a small part of the superb stretch of land between Llandovery and Aberystwyth. Here are the wild tributary valleys of the upper Tywi and the more mountainous parts of Dyfed and it is in this beautiful and mysterious land that many of Britain's rarer birds and animals – the red kite and the polecat and pine marten, for instance – still manage to survive.

CHAPTER EIGHT

Dyffryn Tywi
(The Tywi Valley)

The Afon Tywi, the longest river wholly in Wales, flows down from the moorland uplands of Elennydd through gorges where it meets the harder rocks and then on down in a wide curving lush valley past Llandovery, Llandeilo and Carmarthen to Llansteffan. Rarely is the scenery dramatic and this perhaps is why visitors so often speed along the roads beside the river in a hurry to get to the west coast with little or no time to explore the beauties of this part of Wales. Yet beautiful it is in a serene and peaceful way and despite the apparent lack of mansions, museums and great churches, this, as much as any part, is the heart of Wales in history and spirit. Here for long centuries was the main bastion of the Welsh defence against the Norman advance in the south; for while the princes of Gwynedd in north-western Wales could afford to relax at times far behind the Welsh border the princes of Ystrad Tywi, as the land on either side of the Afon Tywi was known, could never indulge in such a luxury. The stubbornness with which Welsh ways have endured is even testified by medical evidence for here is found the highest incidence in the British Isles of the comparatively rare blood group B, a type usually associated with the survival of Celtic races.

Down the centuries, the agriculturally rich vale has nourished the Welsh spirit, giving rise in the process to many legendary events, until in the latter part of the twentieth century it has, with the advent of Plaid Cymru (the Welsh Nationalist Party) become the political focus of the nation's patriotism.

The headwaters of the Afon Tywi lie in a wild mixture of

moorland, forest and marshes which is inaccessible except on foot. The first crossing of the river by road (from Tregaron to Abergwesyn) is some way down from the source, but visitors who want to explore the main part of the valley must start still further south at Rhandir-mwyn, a pleasant village loosely scattered in a wide arc above a bend of the river. At one time this was an important lead-mining centre and there are still surface workings and ruined buildings to be seen near the village and in the surrounding hills. Now it is the start of a 13-mile-long cul-de-sac to the spectacular Llyn Brianne reservoir. A rock-filled dam, 300 feet high, blocks the entrance to the Tywi gorge to form the reservoir and water is returned to the river either down the adjacent spillway or through a tunnel under the dam to emerge in a great water spout that partly fills the valley with spray. The deep and narrow gorge behind the dam now looks like a Norwegian fjord with steep, forest-clad mountains rising straight out of the water. In part the road runs alongside the reservoir but in other places the rocky sides are so precipitous that the road has been forced to climb higher into the forest and the lake is only then occasionally glimpsed at the many sharp bends. The views everywhere are splendid. It is a sobering thought, nevertheless, that the unchangeability of life and nature which was until recently such a feature of this valley has now, at one fell swoop, been changed forever. It was the wildest of wild places, virtually inaccessible and consequently a wonderful habitat of wild life. Now the sheep farms are uninhabited, the red squirrels and polecats have gone, the red kites and buzzards have flown and instead of old oaks in the valley there are vast areas of coniferous trees on the hillsides. Where once the only sounds heard were the bleating of sheep and the eerie call of birds of prey and Welsh was the only speech known, now all is replaced by the whine of cars and the native tongue has succumbed once again to the demands of progress.

Before the coming of the reservoir the local people went on horseback to chapel at Soar-y-Mynydd in the adjacent Camddwr valley. Possibly the most lonely and remote chapel in Britain, it lies midway between Rhandir-mwyn and Tregaron, both being about ten miles away. But such was the religious fervour of the valley in the early nineteenth century that most of the materials used in the building were carried to the site on horseback over the mountains by the members who lived on farms in the district. The remoteness of the chapel made it necessary to have a small house and stable built alongside to accommodate visiting preachers and their ponies. Remoteness, however, was no bar to enthusiasm; in its heyday all hundred seats would be occupied for services and an *eisteddfod* was held every year in the adjoining field.

Ystrad-ffin, halfway between Llyn Brianne and Rhandir-mwyn is the place associated with the legendary exploits of the sixteenth-century outlaw Twm Sion Catti. To find his hiding place follow the delightful nature trail which starts near the old farmhouse and contines alongside the foaming Tywi to its turbulent confluence with the Afon Doethie. From there a path leads up the steep slopes of Dinas to Ogof Twm Sion Catti, a large cleft in the rocks (not a cave as its name implies) commanding a marvellous view of the rugged valley below. Twm, like Rob Roy, was a picturesque adventurer in his youth but he was also a master of trickery and his escapades always had a flavour of comedy about them. In time the stories attributed to Twm grew and grew and have now become so multifarious that it is almost impossible to distinguish fact from fiction.

He was, however, a real person named Thomas Jones who lived from 1530 to 1610 and was brought up near Tregaron. His favourite haunt seems to have been the upper Tywi Valley and it was here that he met his second wife, the heiress of Ystrad-ffin, whom he married in 1607. Long before that he had, in 1559, received a pardon for hs misdeeds and became a respectable citizen, poet, antiquarian and eventually a magistrate.

A little way up the adjoining Doethie valley the oakwood forest of Allt Rhyd-y-groes is now a National Nature Reserve. A permit is required to visit the reserve for it is only in native oak woods like this and others in nearby tributary valleys that one of Britain's rarest birds, the red kite, manages a precarious survival. The largest bird of prey after the golden eagle, it has a reddish plumage and can be identified easily by its long and distinctive forked tail. Until the nineteenth century this kite was common throughout

Britain, but by about 1870 it had been exterminated in England and Scotland. As late as 1880, it was still fairly common in the Usk Valley, but about that time Scottish gamekeepers were brought into the country estates and the birds were rapidly killed off. By the beginning of the present century the total number of kites, all of which were confined to the Rhandir-mwyn area, was down to less than a dozen and strenuous efforts were then made to protect the bird. At times the efforts seemed doomed to failure either because of severe winters, unscrupulous egg collectors or food poisoning so that in some years only one young bird was successfully bred. The future of this beautiful bird now seems more secure as its range of breeding places has been gradually extended. Even so, there are still probably only about 70 kites in the whole of Wales and constant protection is essential.

Further west the Doethie valley divides into two gorges. Cwm Pysgotwr is a veritable canyon and difficult to penetrate even on foot. The upper Doethie is easier to pass and is interesting for its relics of *tai unnos*. The *tŷ unnos* or 'one-night house', came about as the result of a Welsh custom during the Middle Ages that allowed a man to claim a piece of common land if he could build a house on it between sunset and sunrise. At sunset the man, helped by his friends would start by building the walls, usually of prepared turf. These would then be covered with a thatched roof, leaving a small hole for smoke to escape from the fire which had to be alight by daybreak. After living in the *tŷ unnos* for a year and a day the builder was then allowed to build a permanent dwelling around it and dismantle the turf house from within. In the Doethie valley the *ty unnos* tradition persisted until the middle of the nineteenth century when more than a dozen were built, but all have long since been abandoned and only the foundations of the outer stone houses remain.

Continuing down the Tywi Valley the road to Llandovery passes close to Pont Dolau-hirion, a lovely single-arched bridge built by William Edwards in 1773. Though smaller than Edwards' pioneering bridge at Pontypridd in Glamorgan it is built on the same principle, with a gracefully curved arch and haunches pierced with circular openings. The unspoilt setting adds greatly to the appearance of Pont Dolau-hirion whereas the bridge at Pontypridd is now marred by later development.

Llandovery has a history that goes back to Roman times. The Romans chose this as the site of one of their forts but little now remains to be seen of that apart from some grassy banks on the hill where the venerable old church of Llanfair-ar-y-bryn stands on the northern outskirts of the town. 'St Mary's on the hill' still retains an appearance of immense antiquity and contains some fine timbered roofs despite later restoration. Non-conformists will be drawn to the rather brash red monument in the churchyard marking the grave of William Williams Pantycelyn (1716-1791), the most prolific of Welsh hymn writers and a profound influence on the Methodist Revival during the middle of the eighteenth century. His work is so loved and well known in Wales that it is identified merely by a single 'W' below the right-hand corner of each hymn. The hymns themselves are pure poetry and it is this feeling for and command of words, even when occasionally written in English, such as the famous 'Guide Me, O Thou Great Jehovah', that gives them their irresistable power. Pantycelyn, the farm where Williams lived, lies a short way out of Llandovery off the Brecon road.

Llandovery's other church, known as Llanndigad, stands on the southern side of the town. It dates from the fourteenth century and has a double nave. In an unmarked grave in the churchyard lies the body of Vicar Rhys Prichard, the writer of *Canwyll y Cymry* ('The Welshman's Candle'). This was a book of popular verse and had much the same influence in Wales in the early seventeenth century as John Bunyan's *Pilgrim's Progress* had in England. An apocryphal story relates that Prichard led a somewhat drunken existence in his youth until one day he saw a goat refuse alcohol and realising the significance of this was suddenly converted and set about reproving himself and his flock in rhyme.

Llandovery's main streets are laid out to a square plan, but the overall appearance is rather formless and not particularly attractive, although strangely George Borrow thought it 'about the pleasantest little town in which I have halted in the course of my wanderings'. As one might expect for such a long-established borough the town is full of interest. At one corner of the layout there is the old triangular cobbled market square backed by a plain single-storey market hall and next to it a more imposing town hall over an open arcade.

Nearby is a handsome Georgian house, now Lloyds Bank, but once the Black Ox Bank. It was founded by drovers in 1799 in the days when Llandovery was an important cattle centre. In those days herds of black cattle and sheep would be assembled at convenient places before setting out on their long journeys over rough tracks to the English Midlands and London. The drovers might be several weeks on their journeys and needed to carry large amounts of money. In addition they were often entrusted with handling other people's money. As a result banks for the drovers were set up and issued notes bearing animal symbols (for the use of monoglot Englishmen rather than illiterate Welshmen) denoting their value. The Tregaron bank, for instance, used a picture of a lamb for a ten shilling note, a sheep for £1.00 and two ewes for £2.00. At the Llandovery bank – the last of the drover's banks to survive, until it was taken over in 1909 – notes were illustrated with a black ox and hence the name of the bank.

Like most towns in Wales Llandovery has its castle, in this case the remains of a late thirteenth-century round keep on top of a steep mound. From the town side it is unexceptional but seen from the opposite side of the Afon Bran, a tributary of the Tywi, it looks very picturesque. For a town of its size, Llandovery has an unusually large number of public houses and some good-looking chapels, notably Tabernacle, Salem, Ebenezer and the William Williams Memorial Chapel. It also has a public school, known as Llandovery College, built in watered-down Gothic style in 1848 with money left by Thomas Phillips, a doctor who made his fortune in India. In the College Chapel there is a Crucifixion painting by Graham Sutherland.

The small village of Myddfai to the south-east of Llandovery is famous for its physicians. It lies at the foot of Y Mynydd Du (The Black Mountain or Carmarthen Fan) where in a deep craggy hollow there is a beautiful little lake, Llyn Y Fan Fach, supposedly the home of the lady of the lake. Here, according to the folk story a lake-maiden once fell in love with a farmer and bore him three sons.

119

The farmer, apparently for no reason, struck his wife three times and she returned to the lake taking with her the marriage dowry of sheep and cattle. One day Rhiwallon, the eldest of the three sons, saw his mother again at the lakeside. She told him that his mission in life was to cure the ills and diseases of mankind and showed him where various medicinal herbs and plants grew. Rhiwallen told his brothers of the meeting and with their natural skill and newly acquired knowledge the three sons soon became famous as the Physicians of Myddfai. So much for the legend, but what is curious is that there really was a doctor of Myddfai by the name of Rhiwallon and he was appointed as court physician to Rhys Gryg, the Lord of Dinefwr in the Middle Ages. He had three sons who were also physicians. Two farms locally are named after two brothers Ifan Beddyg and Meredydd Feddyg (Evan the Physician and Meredith the Physician) and one of their descendants, 'David Jones of Mothvey, Surgeon' has a tombstone (dated 1719) in Myddfai Church. Another descendant was a seventeenth-century bishop of Llandaf and so it went on until the last descendant of the Physicians, a Dr C. Rice Williams, of Aberystwyth, died in 1842 at the age of 85. However much one smiles at the old folk stories it is remarkable that a place as small and otherwise insignificant as Myddfai can produce such a notable line of doctors, generation after generation.

Llangadog, a small town or a large village depending on one's standpoint, is the gateway to a fascinating series of lanes and by-ways that meander across the foothills of Y Mynydd Du and which are well worth exploring. There was a *castell* to the south of the village town but nothing can be seen except for some low earthworks. A little way to the south-west is the hamlet of Bethlehem, celebrated for its prized postmark on Christmas stamps, while further along the crest of a steep hill is the astonishingly large hill-fort of Garn Goch fortified with massive ramparts and strategically positioned to command the Vale of Tywi.

Llangadog itself is the home of one of Wales' best known contemporary politicians Gwynfor Evans, lawyer, preacher, farmer and proud leader of Plaid Cymru (Welsh Nationalist Party).

Gwynfor Evans' lifelong aim has been the setting up of a Welsh Parliament which would enable the Welsh nation to make its own decisions on matters affecting it. In a by-election in 1966 the vision of a self-governing Wales was brought a step nearer when he won a momentous victory and became the first Welsh Nationalist to be returned to Westminster. To many in Wales this was perhaps the most important event in Welsh political history since the 1906 General Election when every parliamentary seat in Wales was won by a Liberal pledged to Welsh Home Rule.

On the opposite bank of the Tywi stands Abermarlais, one of several mansions owned by Sir Rhys ap Thomas in the fifteenth century. It was he who led an army from southern Wales in 1485 to join Henry Tudor at the Battle of Bosworth and it was he who, tradition maintains, slew Richard III and thus ensured the crown for the first Tudor King of England. With the Red Dragon banner flying over Bosworth Field and a victorious Welsh claimant to the throne Welshmen could perhaps be forgiven for thinking of the battle as a victory over the English. Within 50 years they were to learn that union with England brought equality only at the sacrifice of their ancient language and culture. Ap Thomas himself was more astute than many and managed to serve the Tudor kings nobly at the same time as he continued to patronise Welsh culture. The bards praised him profusely and when he died Lewis Morgannwg wrote: 'There is no wine, there are no gifts, now that Sir Rhys, prince of this isle, has left us.'

Both Llandovery and Llangadog stand on the east side of the Tywi on separate tributary rivers which have the same name, Afon Bran (River of the Crow). By an odd coincidence the two main tributaries on the west bank of the Tywi in this area are both known as Afon Dulais (River of the Black Voice) and a detour taking in these valleys should not be missed. The northernmost Dulais reaches the Tywi at Llanwrda and from there the road follows the river in a narrow winding valley towards Pumsaint where nearly 2,000 years ago the Romans set up camp and mined gold.

The Ogofau gold mines at Pumsaint lie in a small *cwm* alongside the Cothi valley and have been worked intermittently from probably as far back as the Iron Age up to the 1930's. The remains of a castle motte at the foot of the *cwm* indicate the site's importance in medieval times as well while nearby Carreg Pumsaint, a large upright stone pillar with clear cup-markings on all four sides confirms that the Romans were not the first here. The Romans however mined the area the most intensively, for this was one of their most important mines in Europe, and the present appearance of the little valley is mainly due to their activity. The lower part of the valley was quarried out as an open-cast mine and now forms a large flat-bottomed hollow. Further up the valley the sides are pitted with smaller quarries, caves, tunnel entrances and remains of reservoirs all so weathered and overgrown that it is difficult to make out which are natural and which are man-made. In order to work the mines and wash the gold from the dross the Romans constructed an amazing aqueduct system to supply water to the site. Six miles long, it collected water at the upper end of the Cothi valley and carried it to storage tanks at Ogofau by way of canals following the sides of the valley. The aqueduct system can still be recognised on the open hillside as a series of ledges and banks, but in the afforested areas all traces have been virtually obliterated. The goldmine site, as well as large parts of the beautiful Cothi valley, are now protected by the National Trust and nature trails have been opened for those wishing to explore this very interesting area more fully. The property includes a hotel and a number of small upland farms and was given to the National Trust by Mr H. T. C. Lloyd-Jones as a memorial to the Jones family who had owned the land since the late fifteenth century. One of the more interesting members of this family was Jane Johnes of Dolaucothi who on her secret marriage to Thomas Johnes in 1784 became the mistress of Hafod near Aberystwyth.

The diminutive village of Caeo in the next valley is the religious centre of the district. The church there stands fortress-like on a hill completely dominating the village with its massive grey stone tower. Pumsaint itself has no church although its name signifies an ancient religious site meaning 'five saints'.

After its hectic race down from the mountains to Pumsaint the Cothi suddenly changes course and then sluggishly meanders for a while in a broad vale as far as Edwinsford. The river then becomes a torrent again as it hurries down to pretty Abergorlech with its fine, centuries-old bridge and on through a delightful valley to Brechfa and its forests.

Edwinsford, or Rhydodyn as it was formerly known, is now a picturesque pile with the makings of a superb stage set for a Gothick tale of suspense. The existing mansion dates from the seventeenth century but was extensively altered and added to in both succeeding centuries. The original owners, the Williams family, had a far longer history, claiming descent from the royal house of Deheubarth through the blood of Rhys ap Tewdwr, Hywel Dda and Rhodri Mawr. An elegant bridge built in 1783, leads across the river to the crumbling house and close to there is a charming group of coach-houses and stables dating from 1809.

Southwards the road climbs up through an avenue of oaks and then skirts a lake couplet in an elysian setting at Talley before following the southern Afon Dulais down to the Tywi again at Llandeilo. Talley itself lies off the main road at the head of the two lakes (the name in fact means 'the end of the lakes') in a beautiful secluded setting alongside the gaunt ruins of an abbey. Apart from the abbey's central tower and a few walls little remains above ground because the ruins have been extensively quarried for, among other things, the eighteenth-century parish church, but the general plan of the abbey can be made out. It was founded at the end of the twelfth century by Rhys ap Gruffydd for the Premonstratensians, or White Canons, and was the only house belonging to this order in Wales. Back on the main road Capel Esgairnant, with its round-headed windows and strong quoinwork, stands out as an elegant example of early nineteenth century non-conformist architecture.

Nearer Llandeilo, but hidden away in the hills to the west, is Taliaris, a large seventeenth-century mansion refronted about 1780 in a severe Palladian style facade. Inside, it retains its original Jacobean staircase and there are richly modelled plaster ceilings and fine timber-panelled walls.

Llandeilo, or more correctly, Llandeilo Fawr (Great) to distinguish it from numerous lesser Llandeilos, takes its name from

St Teilo who is reputed to have died here in the sixth century. It was established as a borough by the bishops of Tyddewi in the thirteenth century and is now a pleasant and interesting little market town with narrow streets hugging the slopes of a knoll overlooking a wide bend in the Tywi. At the foot of the hill on which Llandeilo stands, a splendid single-arch bridge spans the river. This was built in 1848 and is the work of David Edwards, son of William Edwards, the famous bridge builder. From the Tywi bridge the round towers of the old castle of Dinefwr can be seen in the distance on the edge of a wooded precipice. With this castle and its successor the history and fate of Llandeilo have been inextricably bound throughout the centuries.

The earliest record of Dinefwr goes back as far as 876 when as the *castell* of Rhodri Mawr it became one of the three royal palaces of Wales. As the capital of Deheubarth, it was of supreme importance in the continuous conflict with the invading Normans (and later between the English and the independent Welsh princes) and as a result was bitterly contested on many occasions. In the late twelfth century when Prince Rhys ap Gruffydd was lord of Deheubarth, Dinefwr was at the peak of its importance. Thereafter the *castell* and the surrounding district were in dispute between lesser princes, who vacillated between supporting the other Welsh princes or siding with the English King. Gradually the independent areas began to disintegrate under the threat of English power until in 1256 Llywelyn ap Gruffydd, prince of Gwynedd, established his supremacy over most of the country and restored Dinefwr to one of his pro-Welsh supporters. The following spring King Henry III, incensed by these events, sent Stephan Bauzen to Carmarthen to regain Ystrad Tywi. The English army set out from Carmarthen on 31 May to capture Dinefwr but three days later they were annihilated at Coed Llathen when 3,000 English soldiers, including their leader Bauzen, were killed. For nearly 20 years Dinefwr stayed safely in Welsh hands until in 1276 it fell once more to the English and this time, apart from a brief revolt in 1287, it remained a foreign garrison.

Alongside the Welsh *castell* there had been a small Welsh borough. In 1298 Edward I established a new borough, known as

Y Drenewydd (New Town), to the north so that by the thirteenth century there were, including Llandeilo, three small boroughs side by side. Llandeilo progressed but the two Dinefwr boroughs were overwhelmed in the fifteenth century when a large mansion and gardens were built on the site. In 1660 the mansion was rebuilt and this with various extension and alterations, including a Victorian Gothic refronting is the house that stands today. The large park which surrounds the old *castell* and the mansion was landscaped in the late eighteenth century by Capability Brown. It is of especial interest both for the herds of shy fallow deer which graze there and for its rare and attractive white cattle (one of only five herds in Britain today) which are thought to be descendants of the extinct aurochs or giant wild oxen.

Castell Dinefwr was but one of a trio of important Welsh castles that controlled the rich Dyffryn Tywi. The most magnificently sited of the three is Castell Carreg Cennen perched on the very edge of a 300-foot precipice overlooking a narrow defile in the Cennen valley to the south-east of Llandeilo. From the hamlet of Trapp further down the valley the *castell* stands out in striking silhouette above limestone cliffs; approaching it by road, from the rear as it were, the effect is less dramatic though it still forms a good skyline. Most of the original Welsh structure has been obscured by later additions built by the English lords at the end of the thirteenth century and the inside of the fortress is a mere shell, somewhat disappointing after the splendour suggested by the exterior. It does, however, have one unusual feature that ought not to be missed. This is the cliff passage leading from the inner ward to a natural cave in the mountain. Narrow openings in the outer wall of the passage enable one to look down from the top of the cliff to the valley below, but the cave itself is long and dark so that a torch is necessary.

Castell Dryslwyn, the third of the trio of Welsh castles, stands on an isolated hill next to the Tywi. From the road the remains of the castle, uncared for since the days when it vied with Dinefwr for supremacy of Ystrad Tywi, appear scant and unrewarding but a scramble to the top of the hill will reveal sizeable ruins and large earthworks. From the top one can look back up the Vale and see

Castell Dinefwr in the distance and nearer at hand Y Grongaer, the hill celebrated since the early eighteenth century by poets and painters alike but most of all by John Dyer in his poem 'Grongar Hill'. Dyer lived at the now derelict mansion of Aberglasney nearby. On the opposite side of the Tywi one can make out the walls of Gelli Aur (Golden Grove), once the historic home of the Vaughan family but rebuilt as a Gothic castle in 1827 and now a farm institute, and beyond the craggy outline of Castell Carreg Cennen.

Nearer to the south-west, the skyline is conspicuously broken by Paxton's tower, a peculiar triangular structure with castellated round turrets at each corner and a tower containing a banqueting room in the centre. It was ostensibly erected in honour of Lord Nelson, but a less generous explanation relates that Sir William Paxton built the useless folly in a fit of petulance when he failed to get elected as MP for the district. The tower has been restored by the National Trust and is worth visiting for the superb panoramic view of the valley all the way from Ystrad-ffin down to Carmarthen. In the centre of the panorama theTywi meanders lazily through a dead flat plain and Dryslwyn hill stands out like an island in the midde distance.

The unusual flatness of the Tywi valley compared with the abrupt steepness of the hills on either side ensures that even comparatively small hills near the river make marvellous viewpoints. A good example at the lower end of the vale is Llangunnor, where from a small isolated thirteenth-century church on top of the hill one can look straight down into Carmarthen town, just across the river, or inland as far as Dryslwyn. The poet Sir Lewis Morris and the hymnist David Charles are buried here and Richard Steele, founder of the *Tatler* and the *Spectator* in the eighteenth century, had his estates nearby and has a memorial tablet in the church.

To the east of Abergwili, on the north bank of the river, Merlin's Hill (or more correctly Brynmyrddin, for this is the reported burial place of Myrddin the enchanter of the Arthurian legends) is another place for superb vistas.

Abergwili is today almost a suburb of Carmarthen but still

retains its own historic identity. In 1020 Llywelyn ap Seisyll won a famous battle here that confirmed his position as ruler of Dyfed, Gwynedd and Powys and as the Prince of Wales a century before the Normans arrived in this part of Britain. In the sixteenth century Bishop Barlow transferred the bishop's palace from Tyddewi (St David's) to Abergwili, in order to be nearer the civilised life of Carmarthen. Not all bishops were able to share his view of the town's gentility. A few years later in 1555 Bishop Ferrar was burnt at the stake in front of Carmarthen Castle and became one of the first Welsh martyrs since Roman times. The next incumbent of the palace, Bishop Richard Davies, took care not to offend anyone and together with William Salesbury of Llanrwst made the first translation of the *New Testament* and the *Book of Common Prayer* into Welsh. Most of the Bishop's Palace was burnt down in 1903 – only the seventeenth-century Laud's Chapel surviving the disaster – and has since been rebuilt.

In 1109 when King Henry I built his castle on the cliff overlooking Carmarthen bridge and established a new town there he was merely repeating an exercise in strategic planning which had been done twice before. In the first century the Romans chose Carmarthen (Moridunum) to be one of their main fortresses in Wales. This stronghold, guarding the Tywi estuary and controlling the route into western Wales, was somewhere in the area of present-day Priory Street and seems to have had attached to it a considerable civil settlement or town. After the withdrawal of the Romans a Celtic church was established in roughly the same area by St Teulyddog (a disciple of St Teilo) and gradually a settlement gathered around this too. Old Carmarthen, as the Celtic town later came to be known, survived as a separate entity alongside the English town of New Carmarthen until 1546, when the two were combined to form the largest and most important borough in Wales.

Of the Norman castle very little remains apart from the great gateway hidden away behind later buildings, facing Nott Square. The castle had a tempestuous history, being attacked and captured by the Welsh, notably by Glyndŵr in 1403 and 1405, on many occasions. The site of its quadrangular courtyard has, since 1939, been occupied by a great château-like office block of the county council. Before that it was the site of a county gaol designed by John Nash. To the west of the castle in Bridge Street a short length of the earliest town wall, erected in 1233, still stands and eastwards behind Dan y Banc there is another length of town wall dating from the period when New Carmarthen was extended at the beginning of the fifteenth century.

St Peter's, the parish church of Carmarthen, stands in a traffic island midway between what were once the old and new towns. The fact that it was outside the English walled town suggests that there was a church here long before the Normans came, but the present structure is mostly fourteenth- to sixteenth-century work in the Perpendicular style. Inside there is the massive tomb of Sir Rhys ap Thomas, the hero of Bosworth Field.

Further east at the end of Priory Street a forlorn and withered stump of an old oak tree still manages to stand upright in a last determined effort to save Carmarthen from oblivion, for in a prophecy which legend attributes to Myrddin (Merlin) the magician, 'when this oak shall tumble down, so will fall Carmarthen town'. The ominous prediction is taken more seriously than one might suppose for the very name Carmarthen (in Welsh, Caerfyrddin) means 'Myrddin's Fort' and as a result the venerable oak has been assiduously preserved and bolstered up with concrete and guarded by iron railings. Even to the most optimistic, however, its days must appear to be numbered. Opposite the old oak is the site of an Augustinian priory where in 1105 *Llyfr Ddu Caerfyrddin* ('The Black Book of Carmarthen'), the oldest book in the Welsh language, was written. The manuscript is now in the National Library at Aberystwyth.

Carmarthen has always been an important administrative and market centre and today it is busier than ever. The shopping and commericial centre which was originally focused in Notȝ Square outside the castle has now extended eastwards along King Street to St Peter's Church and westwards down the hill past the handsome Guildhall (built in 1767) to Dark Gate and Lammas Street. The Museum in Quay Street near the Guildhall is housed in a Georgian building and has a good archaeological collection, including a number of stones with Ogham inscriptions. The town also has a large number of chapels varying in appearance from the drab and mundane to one of oustanding excellence. This latter is the English Baptist in Lammas Street which was designed by the local architect George Morgan in 1872 with a great columned portico set back from the street.

Beyond Lammas Street, at a spot where in times past public hangings took place, the tall Picton Monument catches the eye. General Thomas Picton, who was killed at Waterloo in 1815 after a distinguished career as a soldier, was not a native of Carmarthen but had close connections with the town and when the memorial was built his medals were buried beneath it. Other notables closely associated with the town were General William Nott, of India fame (his statue is in Nott Square), John Nash the architect (who lived and practised in Francis Terrace for a dozen years after his fall from grace in London) and Brinley Richards, a friend of Chopin and composer of 'God Bless the Prince of Wales', The latter was born in Hall Street, near the Guildhall, in 1817.

Westwards of Carmarthen a broad vale extends almost as far as St Clears and then turns southwards to meet the coast on the edge of the Taff estuary. A casual observer might expect the Afon Tywi to flow through this vale but it does not; instead it turns directly south at Carmarthen, meanders a short way and is then caught in a restricted passage between the enclosing hills before it emerges again as a broad estuary at Llansteffan and joins with the Taf to disgorge its waters in the sea. It is almost as though the Tywi, now tidal, had been surprised at Carmathen and then lost its way. The countryside below Carmarthen is thus quite different from that seen before and all the villages and roads seem to have hidden themselves behind the shelter of gentle hills.

Llansteffan, on the thick wedge of land between the Tywi and Taf estuaries, is a charmingly peaceful village. The Green, with its terraces of white-washed cottages stands by the edge of the estuary overlooking the great stretches of golden sand while the main part of the village is set back at the foot of a hill. The main street slopes gently up to the church and on past the Plas, an eighteenth-century Grecian-style mansion, and finally curves back towards the estuary where it stops outside the entrance to the thirteenth-century castle. The castle, though strikingly impressive when seen from below and for that reason a favourite with painters, is ruined as a result of its chequered history. Nevertheless, it makes an excellent vantage point to view the surrounding hills, estuaries and peninsulas.

No description of this part of Wales would be complete without mentioning Laugharne and Whitland, the former for its literary associations and the latter for its historical connections. Once it was possible to go westwards from Llansteffan to the eastern side of the Afon Taf and there get a ferry across the estuary to Laugharne. The ferry no longer runs and therefore to get to Laugharne one has first to go northwards through Llanybri with its ruined church (last used as a non-conformist chapel) to St Clears, a straggling town which once possessed a castle and priory (now both visible only as earthen mounds).

Four main roads meet at St Clears and traffic is as much a cause for concern now as it was in the early nineteenth century when the town became one of the chief centres of the Rebecca Riots. For two years the district and eventually the whole of Dyffryn Tywi, was in a seething ferment over abuses of the turnpike trust system which required travellers to pay heavy tolls to use the turnpike roads. The rioters dressed as women and taking their name from a biblical quotation – "the seed of Rebecca shall possess the gates of their adversaries"–systematically burnt down the toll gates and generally created as much chaos to the system as possible. In June 1843 300 men on horseback and some 2,000 more on foot marched on Carmarthen to present a petition to the magistrates, but the demonstration got out of hand and they ended by ransacking the workhouse. Eventually the riots ended when a Commission of Inquiry led to better conditions, but there was still much bitterness and two of the leaders of the riots, Shoni Sgubor Fawr and Dai'r Cantwr, were transported to Tasmania for life.

Laugharne (pronounced Larn) is another charming and interesting coastal town, set where two small valleys meet between two headlands on the shores on the Taf estuary. The main street winds down one side to the valley bottom near the marshy foreshore and then winds up again on the other side away from the sea. Laugharne was chartered as a borough as far back as 1307 and still has its Portreeve and a delectable eighteenth-century town hall complete with white tower and belfry. There are also remains of two castles; Laugharne Castle near the sea, rebuilt as a mansion in the sixteenth century but now a picturesque ruin, and fragments of Roche Castle, further inland.

It is not surprising that such an enchanting town has attracted writers and poets. Amongst them were Ernest Rhys and Richard Hughes, but it was Dylan Thomas, best known of modern Welsh poets, who was most closely associated with Laugharne. Here Thomas settled and lived in the Boathouse overlooking the 'heron-priested shore' until his death in 1954. *Under Milk Wood*, his most famous work, captured for posterity the atmosphere of a small Welsh seaside town such as Laugharne. At the time both poet and residents denied the similarity, but now despite the protestations of many against Dylan Thomas's colourful portrayal of his own people, the town proudly remembers his name every three years with a festival which includes a performance of *Under Milk Wood*. The poet's grave is a simple mound with nothing more than a plain white cross to mark it, in the parish churchyard on the hill at the edge of the town.

Laugharne was also the home in the eighteenth century of one Madame Bevan, chief supporter of Griffith Jones and his famous circulating schools. The Rev. Jones was rector of nearby Llanddowror and from there about 1730, with the financial aid of Madame Bevan, he launched a campaign to educate the ordinary people by sending out scholars to every parish for three-monthly stints to teach both children and adults to read. From these simple beginnings a zest for learning was fostered in Wales which has never ebbed. One consequence of Jones' revolution in learning was the introduction in 1889 of an Education Act establishing secondary schools in Wales 13 years before a similar system was adopted in England.

South of Laugharne a firm, hard beach backed by extensive sand dunes stretches westwards for six miles to Pendine. The old village of Pendine with its gable-towered church, stands high up some way inland. The modern village crouches despairingly below the cliffs, its appearance utterly desecrated by caravans and the bric-a-brac of uncontrolled development, while in high summer the sands themselves at this end are overrun by cars. Massive development by the War Office has not helped to improve a potentially magnificent area. Between the two World Wars the sands at Pendine were the scene of heroic attacks on the land speed record by the Welsh ace Parry Thomas, who was killed in the attempt, and by Sir Malcolm Campbell. The sands were also used by Amy and Jim Mollison as the starting point of their flight across the Atlantic to Newfoundland.

Whitland has little to show now for its contribution to Welsh life and learning, yet it is a famous name in the annals of the nation's history. The fragmentary ruins of its twelfth-century abbey, for instance, are of little architectural interest, but historically they are of especial importance as being the remains of the first Cistercian abbey in Wales. The abbey was founded directly from the Continent and from it in turn most of the other Cistercian abbeys in Wales were derived. Of all the monastic orders the Cistercians with their ascetic ideals seem to have fitted in best with the native religious traditions and consequently they were warmly supported by the princes. It was in these abbeys that much of the medieval history of Wales was recorded and many of the heroes of Wales were buried.

The Welsh name for Whitland is Hendy-gwyn which in turn is a reference to Ty Gwyn ar Daf ('White House on the Taf') where about the year 930 Hywel Dda (Howell the Good), king of Wales, summoned a great meeting to consolidate the laws of different parts of Wales into a single and comprehensive legal system. Both clergy and laymen took part in the assembly and the result was an astonishing legal code that in many ways was more advanced than anything similar in Europe at the time. They incorporated, for instance, the first known building regulations in Britain, including stringent fire precautions. Indeed, some of the principles of Hywel's code, such as equality for women, have only been adopted in English law during the present century.

Hywel was not only an exceptionally able legislator and administrator but he was also an astute politician. He saw both

Wales and England in European terms as nations sharing traditions common with other Latinised peoples and not those of the Teutonic tribes. It was this outlook that made him refuse to take part in a Celtic-Scandinavian alliance to overthrow Anglo-Saxon England, a combined assault from which England could hardly have recovered at that period. With a strong and powerful Britain dominated by Scandinavian Norsemen it is doubtful if William, Duke of Normandy, could have so easily conquered England a century later. Hywel was not to know how disastrously Wales would suffer from the Normans in succeeding centuries, but even so his decision not to help in the obliteration of his weakened Anglo-Saxon neighbour may well, in the long run, have saved the whole of Britain and much of Europe from a return to paganism.

CHAPTER NINE

The South Pembrokeshire Coast

The first place of any importance on arriving from the east in what used to be the old county of Pembrokeshire is Narberth, a compact market town with a slightly Georgian flavour. There is little to see in the small town itself apart from its attractive little town hall complete with the Royal Coat of Arms, but immediately south there are extensive but very ruinous remains of a Norman castle. The castle from which the town takes its name, Castell yn Arberth, once dominated the district, protecting those to the south and discouraging those to the north. It is noticeable that nearly all the place names south of Narberth are English, for this is the start of the area known rather naively as 'Little England beyond Wales', while place names to the north are predominantly Welsh. Long before the coming of the Normans, who built the castle, and the Flemings, who garrisoned it, Narberth was well known to the Princes of Dyfed who, according to the *Mabinogion* had one of their courts there.

The district round about is pleasant but lacks the dramatic qualities of the coastal areas and consequently most visitors speed on westwards to Haverfordwest or southwards to Tenby without stopping to explore. This is a pity for just north of the A40 road Llawhaden has an interesting bishop's castle standing high up above a densely wooded bank. The castle dates from the late thirteenth century and was built by the immensely rich bishops of St David's as one of their fortified mansions. Though ruined the castle still retains its moat and an impressive gateway and commands good views across the valley. Llawhaden village is sited on the high ground behind the castle, but the curious double-towered church, an elaborate eighteenth-century water mill and the medieval bridge lie picturesquely together in the valley below.

Saundersfoot is just to the east of the main road to Tenby. Its main attractions are the excellent sandy beaches on either side of the harbour around which the village is built. The harbour was constructed for the export of anthracite coal in the early nineteenth century, but is now packed with sailing boats. Coal is no longer extracted and except for the pleasant footpath on the site of the old colliery tramway to Wiseman's Bridge there is little outward sign of the industry ever having existed here. Hean Castle, on the hill to the north was, nevertheless, built with the profits from coal and is barely a century old.

Tenby must rate highly as the most attractive of all seaside resorts in Wales. In fact it would stand comparison with the best anywhere, for the view of the town across the harbour is magnificent. The visual attractiveness of the place is partly due to its exceptionally fine site on a headland jutting out between fine sandy beaches and ending in the Castle Hill peninsula and partly to the intrinsic character of its buildings and its charming street layout. Though Dinbych-y-Pysgod ('Little fort of the fishes'), as it is otherwise known, was recorded as long ago as the ninth century in a Welsh poem the town's development did not really start until the Normans arrived and built their fortress on Castle Hill. Only the barest fragments of the castle now remain, although one of the halls now houses an interesting local museum. The town walls were first built in the thirteenth century and eventually completely surrounded the town, even along the top of the cliffs. The cliff walls have gone but on the landward side the walls, including half a dozen towers, are virtually intact and still stand to their full height. By the eighteenth century Tenby had begun to go into decline and it was not until the 1760's that the growing popularity of sea-bathing gave it a new lease of life. A local magnate, Sir William Paxton, taking advantage of the current vogue, ploughed money into improving the town at the beginning of the nineteenth century and it then became a fashionable watering place. It was Paxton who built the public baths (now Laston House) in Castle Square and appropriately embellished the entrance with the Greek inscription: 'the sea washes away all the ills of the world'.

Old Tenby within the walls still retains its winding street and steep lanes, but most of the medieval buildings have been replaced by later work. The most prominent building is St Mary's Church in the High Street, its tall spire standing out in silhouette head and shoulders above the rest of the town. Built in the thirteenth century and extensively added to in the two succeeding centuries it is the largest medieval parish church in Wales, and though plainish externally it is spacious and full of interest inside. Above the chancel and the elegant nave arcade, for instance, there is a superb panelled waggon-roof ceiling with 69 bosses at the intersections skilfully carved with humorous designs. The sanctuary at the end of the chancel is raised unusually high above the level of the rest of the church so that it has to be approached by a broad flight of steps. There are a number of good monuments to local notables but perhaps the most interesting is the seventeenth-century medallion commemorating Robert Recorde, the inventor (if such an unexciting fact can be called an invention) of the mathematical symbol for equality. He was born in Tenby in 1510 and was well known in his day as an author of works on medicine and astronomy as well as mathematics.

Tenby was also the home of the artists Augustus and Gwen John. Augustus himself was born in a house in the Esplanade in 1878, but his sister Gwen was born two years earlier in Haverfordwest. Both, however, were brought up in Tenby and it is here that they shared their first studio. As artists and as people brother and sister were entirely different in outlook. Augustus John, the more famous of the two, had an immense zest for life and friendship and stood out as the Bohemian artist *par excellence*. He was moreover an exceptionally good portrait painter as well as a brilliant draughtsman and vigorous landscapist. Gwen John on the other hand was by contrast reticent to a degree and limited her painting to a few subjects close to her heart, but they always had a rare refinement and grace.

In Tudor Square, alongside a narrow stepped alley, is the old Tudor Merchant's House, an interesting survivor from the fifteenth century when Tenby was an important fishing port. Its three-storeyed gable walls with corbelled chimney incorporating a large window, gives the building a suitable antique charm from the outside, while inside much of the old timber flooring and some of the original painted wall decoration remains. The house has been restored by the National Trust and the lower floors are open to the public. Next door is a Plantagenet House, another fifteenth-century house owned by the National Trust and used as a restaurant.

St Julian's Chapel next to the harbour is a much altered building of no great age which replaced an earlier chapel which once stood at the end of the pier. Known also as the Fisherman's Church it has now a perhaps too obvious nautical character inside which it almost certainly never had when fishermen used to attend services before taking their boats out to sea.

Two notable islands stand offshore. St Catherine's Island, the smaller of the two, lies just beyond Castle Hill and is accessible on foot at low tide. Long flights of steps lead up the cliffside to a massive mid-nineteenth century fort built to defend potential landing places on the Pembroke peninsula. It once had an armament of eleven large guns but more recently it has been used as a zoo.

Caldy, the larger of the two islands lies less than a mile south of Giltar Point and Penally. Of all the islands within the bounds of the Pembrokeshire Coast National Park this is the most fertile and the one with the most continuous history. It is also the most accessible, there being frequent boat trips (about half an hour each way) from Tenby in the summer. The ferry-boat beaches at Priory Bay on the island's northern side and from there visitors can explore the island provided they keep to the well-marked footpaths. Having had strong Christian connections for so long most of the island's interesting features are to do with religion and the monastic community which owns and farms the land. From the beach the main path goes upwards towards a medieval circular watchtower and a modern Calvary high on the top of the cliffs and then past a pleasant fishpond to Caldy village and the imposing Cistercian monastery of Our Lady and St Sampson. The monastery was started in 1907 for an Anglican community, but before it was finished the monks decided to follow the Benedictine rule as Catholics. In 1928 most of them moved to Prinknash in Gloucestershire and the following year Caldy came into possession of the Belgian abbey of Chimay. The modern monastery and abbey church stand on a slight hill and form a spectacular group of white buildings with high red-tile roofs. They were designed by the Cardiff architect Coates Carter in Rhenish Romanesque style, with great semi-circular arches on the ground floor and narrow slit windows to the floors above. All can visit the interior of the abbey church but the conducted tour of the monastery is for men only. A heavily restored Romanesque church (St David's) stands in front of the monastery along with a tea garden, refreshment room and shops selling the abbey's products, particularly the perfumes for which the monks are famous.

Beyond the monastery and almost in the centre of the island is the ancient priory which was built as a dependent of St Dogmael's Abbey in the early twelfth century. Though tiny, it is the most complete medieval monastery in Wales and still retains, remarkably intact, various buildings grouped in a square around the minute cloister garth. The priory church has a peculiar weather-worn leaning spire on top of its corbelled tower and inside there are stone-vaulted roofs and cobbled floors. A richly coloured and beautiful stained-glass window of St Illtud, by Dom Theodore Bailey, lights the south wall of the nave. Nearby stands a stone pillar with Latin and Ogham inscriptions, a physical link with Caldy's first monastery founded by Celtic monks probably in the sixth century on the same site as the medieval priory. Another link with the past is through St Sampson, one of the first Celtic abbots of Caldy and later first bishop of Dol in Brittany. In a touching tribute the Benedictine monks brought a small part of Sampson's relics back from Dol to Caldy in 1919 and dedicated their new monastery to his name.

Manorbier, the home of one of Wales' most famous sons, lies just to the south of the main road from Tenby to Pembroke. A steep valley drops down from the village to a fine sandy bay and midway between the two are the ancient parish church on one side of the valley and Manorbier Castle on the other side. The splendid castle stands proudly on a ridge above the road like some great Crusader castle in Syria, but it took little part in any wars. Though privately owned it is open to the public and well worth a visit, especially to see the Round Tower. Much of the interior has been restored and some rooms are dressed up with effigies (from Madame Tussauds) of some of the people who once inhabited the castle and now perhaps haunt it. Most of the existing fabric of the castle dates from the thirteenth and early fourteenth century, but there was a fortress on the site at least a century earlier and it was in this earlier redoubt that the illustrious and remarkable Gerald de Barri was born in 1146.

Giraldus Cambrensis (Gerald of Wales) as he is popularly known, was the son of William de Barri, a Norman noble, and grandson of Nest, the Welsh 'Helen of Troy' and daughter of the last independent Prince of Deheubarth. Giraldus was a tempestuous figure in a turbulent age and though only half Welsh – 'I am sprung from the princes of Wales and the barons of the Marches, and when I see injustice in either race I hate it' – he struggled thoughout his life to assert the independence of the Welsh Church from Canterbury and Norman domination. After distinguishing himself as a scholar at university in Paris he returned to Wales to become Archdeacon of Brecon. His ambition, however, was to become Bishop of St David's and when a few years later his uncle Bishop David died, most assumed that Gerald would take his place. He had in fact been in charge of the administration of the diocese for some time and it therefore seemed right and proper for him to take over completely. The chapter nominated Gerald for the post and then made a fatal mistake, for without waiting for the King's approval to the nomination Gerald was acclaimed and Te Deums were sung in the churches. Henry II was furious at having had his consent taken for granted, but worse he considered that Gerald, as a descendent of the royal house of Wales, was political dynamite. He therefore refused even to consider him for the vacancy. Twice again during Gerald's lifetime the see of St David's became vacant, but despite three perilous journeys to Rome he was overruled by the English King and Canterbury. Embittered both with the English and the Welsh, whom he thought had let him down, Gerald retired to France. Perhaps if he had been less open about his ambitions and his heartfelt wish to make the Welsh Church answerable only to Rome, he might have succeeded better; as it was he was greatly respected as a scholar and was offered a number of bishoprics in Ireland and at Bangor and Llandaf, all of which he politely declined.

The fame of Giraldus Cambrensis, however, rests more with his pioneeering geographical essays, which he wrote in his early years, than with his fight to keep the Welsh church independent. In 1185 he accompanied Prince John to Ireland and collected material for his first two books, the *Topography of Ireland* and *Conquest of Ireland*. Three years later he was the companion of Archbishop Baldwin when he toured Wales to preach the Third Crusade. From the material gained on this journey he wrote the famous *Itinerary through Wales* and *Description of Wales*. At the time that the two latter books were written, Giraldus had not yet fallen foul of the English clergy and he tended to be more pro-Norman than pro-Welsh. Even so, he was at pains to show his impartiality and the last chapters of the *Description* are entitled: 'In what manner this nation (of Wales) is to be overcome' and 'In what manner this nation may resist and revolt'. In spite of some questionable facts in these books, they were nevertheless the first serious accounts written of Wales and Ireland and have now become main sources for the histories of these two countries in the Middle Ages.

Lamphey, on the road to Pembroke has the ruins of one of the bishops of St David's country palaces. The Palace grounds are approached by way of a shady drive with exotic plants to Lamphey Court (a fine late-Georgian mansion) and then through an opening in a high wall. The first part of the palace one sees, and the best preserved, is an isolated gatehouse tower built in the fourteenth century. Beyond is the Palace itself, with the remains of a thirteenth-century hall in the centre and later, large extensions at either end. The most interesting part is the fourteenth-century great hall at the eastern end; this was built with unusual arcaded parapets by Bishop Gower in similar style to his other great palace at St David's. Before any of these buildings were erected there was a timber palace on the site. This was the one referred to

by Giraldus Cambrensis when relating the story of how his grandfather Gerald de Windsor deceived the Welsh by an artful ruse and thus saved Pembroke. De Windsor was Constable of the newly-built castle and according to Giraldus, when the Norman invaders were besieged in the war of 1096 he sent a fake letter to his overlord intending it to fall into the hands of Bishop Wilfred at Lamphey Palace 'as if accidently dropped', stating that they had plenty of provisions and would not require any outside assistance for a least four months. Poor Wilfred, acting in what he thought was the best interest, for he was very much on the side of his compatriots, passed the letter on to the Welsh leaders. Discouraged by the 'news' they abandoned the siege and left Pembroke to the Normans. The bishop was not forgiven for his part in helping the Welsh and was soon forcibly replaced by a Norman bishop.

His stratagem having worked, de Windsor then 'in order to make himself and his dependents more secure, married Nest, the sister of Gruffydd, prince of South Wales, by whom he had an illustrious progeny of both sexes; and by whom the maritime parts of South Wales were retained by the English, and the walls of Ireland afterwards stormed'. Thus are empires made, but how far Princess Nest willingly acquiesced in mothering the children of a Norman baron one can only guess. Perhaps it was to clear the stain on her character that she later ran away with one Welsh prince, and, after de Windsor died, married another.

Pembroke town proper consists of one very long street, unenterprisingly called Main Street, on a narrow peninsula between two branches of the Pembroke river. One end of Main Street is dominated by a rather forbidding classical chapel and the far end is completely overshadowed by the round towers and walls of Pembroke Castle, one of the strongest medieval fortresses in Wales.

The castle stands on a great limestone rock, more than half surrounded by water, at the point of the peninsula. On this tremendous strong-point the Normans built their first castle in timber at the end of the eleventh century and then rebuilt it in stone with an enormous round keep tower and inner ward in the late twelfth century, finally completing it with the outer ward and an elaborately powerful gatehouse in the following century. One of the more curious features is an immense natural cavern, the Wogan Cave, immediately under the inner courtyard which was connected directly to the river on the north side to ensure that the castle could be supplied from the sea in times of need. Because of its well-nigh impregnable position and exceptional strength Pembroke Castle was comparatively little affected in any wars until besieged and then sacked by Oliver Cromwell and his Parliamentarian army in the Civil War.

After Caernarfon, Pembroke is the castle most closely connected with British royalty in Wales and also, somewhat ironically, one of the castles most closely associated with the unification of both Ireland and Wales with England. In the late twelfth century it was, under Richard 'Strongbow', the springboard for the Norman invasion of the 'emerald isle' and in 1210 King John stayed at the castle on his way to unite the Lordship of Ireland with the English Crown and 'with the common consent of all men of Ireland ordained that the laws and customs of the realm of England should be kept therein'. The King must have had considerable nerve to take on Ireland when he still had little more than a few footholds, albeit strong and important footholds, in Wales for at that time Llywelyn the Great still ruled over the larger part of the country, the ancient laws of Hywel Dda still applied in Welsh Wales and key Norman stongholds such as Cardigan, Carmarthen and Montgomery were soon to be overwhelmed and restored to Welsh rule.

There was to be a still greater irony three centuries later when in 1536 Henry VIII, the son of a Welshman born in Pembroke Castle, set in motion the Act of Union of Wales with England, thus striking the deathblow to his own nation's national future. The Welshman born at Pembroke was, of course, Henry Tudor the future King Henry VII, and though Welsh by descent on his father's side, the place of his birth was almost accidental. In 1453 Jasper Tudor, the son of Owain Tudor and Catherine of France, became Earl of Pembroke. Three years later Edmund, the brother of Jasper, sent his 15 year-old wife Margaret Beaufort to Pembroke for safety during the Wars of the Roses and there soon after the death of Edmund at Carmarthen she gave birth to Henry Tudor, Earl of

Richmond, in January 1457. Henry's childhood was spent at Pembroke Castle, but when in 1471 Henry VI and his son Edward died and he became the chief claimant to the throne on his mother's side, Richard III usurped the royal seat and young Henry Tudor was forced to flee to Brittany with his uncle Jasper. Fourteen years later, Henry decided to make an attempt to overthrow the usurper and after first appealing to his countrymen in Wales he returned, landing on the shores of Milford Haven. After marching through Wales to Bosworth Field under the banner of the red dragon he defeated Richard III and thus became the first Welsh King on the English throne.

The whole of the peninsula on which Pembroke stands was enclosed with stout walls, part of which remain on the south side of the town overlooking the park. The three gates that led into the town have gone, although fragments of the arch of one of these can still be seen at the end of an interesting row of old houses just opposite the entrance to the castle. Another gate stood across the road leading northwards to the Mill Bridge, a favourite artist's viewpoint of the castle for centuries. Here a dam holds back the waters of the river to form a lake now used for boating but originally part of the town's defence system.

The most interesting church in Pembroke is at Monkton Priory just outside the old town to the south-west. Very little now remains of the Benedictine priory, which fell into decay after the Reformation, except the church itself with its long, high Romanesque nave, a loftily spacious chancel (restored in the nineteenth century) and a tall, thin tower. Nearby is Monkton Old Hall, built in the fourteenth or fifteenth century and thus one of the oldest inhabited houses in the area. It was presumably originally the prior's house.

North-east of Pembroke, at the end of a creek of the Milford Haven, is the stately grey-white limestone shell of Carew Castle. The castle belonged at first to the Welsh princes but was given by Rhys ap Tewdwr to his daughter Nest when she married Gerald de Windsor. It is roofless now except for some basement rooms in the towers and chapel which still retains a groined cross-vaulted ceiling. Much of the castle was rebuilt in Tudor times and this

145

accounts for its palace-like character when compared with the grim defensive appearance of most castles. The astonishingly large, slender columned windows of the northern wing were, for instance, added in the sixteenth century. Nothing seems to have been spared in order to make this one of the best and most up-to-date mansions of its time, and there was even a piped water supply to the kitchen and brewhouse. Even in ruins the castle appears magnificent and it is not difficult to imagine the colour and splendour of life during its heyday, such as on the occasion in 1507 when Sir Rhys ap Thomas held a great tournament lasting five days to celebrate his appointment as a Knight of the Garter.

Near the entrance to Carew Castle a superb Celtic high-cross stands rather uncomfortably in a small enclosure at the side of the road. More than 14 feet high, it is one of the finest examples of Celtic ornamentation in Wales and is inscribed in Latin to 'King Maredudd, son of Edwin', and ruler of Deheubarth until his death in 1035.

Another place of special interest is Bosherston's famous lily-ponds near the coast south of Pembroke. The lily-ponds (really a trident-shaped lake formed by a sand-bar at the seaward end of the wooded valley) can be reached by a short walk down a rough lane near Bosherston Church. The scenery is at its most colourful during spring and early summer when the lilies are out, but at any time of the year the place is idyllic. Narrow causeway-type bridges cross each arm of the lake to footpaths on the eastern side which lead across Stackpole Warren to secluded Barafundle Bay (no amenities, no cars, but plenty of sand), or alongside the water to the sea at Broadhaven, a splendid sandy beach with a background of cliffs and dunes. A quicker way to Broadhaven (not to be confused, by the way, with the larger place of that name west of Haverfordwest) is by road from Bosherston to the car park at Trefalun where there is another deep valley with great sand cliffs and another small lake.

The coastal scenery to the west of Broadhaven is amongst the most magnificent in the whole of Dyfed, although unfortunately the area is used as part of a tank range (hence the German and English signs in the vicinity) and access is limited to those days when firing is not in progress. The tiny Celtic chapel of St Govan is here spectacularly situated amongst the cliffs in a rocky defile that looks almost like a vast roofless hall opening on to the sea at one end and guarded by two pillars of rock at the corners. The original hermit's cell was cut into the bare rock but in the later chapel (eleventh to fourteenth century) stone 'as found' on the site was used and so matches exactly the colour of the surrounding rocks. Below the chapel there is a holy well, now blocked up by fallen boulders, and below that a natural arch in the cliffs.

Further west the flat-topped cliff scenery becomes more and more dramatic. First there is Boshmere – one of 'ye divers wonders of Pembrokeshire' according to George Owen in the sixteenth century – where two blowholes, connected underground to the sea, spout up volumes of water during south-westerly gales. Then there is the Huntsman's Leap, a narrow chasm in the precipitous cliffs which takes its name from the huntsman who once leapt across on his horse and then died of fright when he looked back to see what he had done. Further along are the Elugug Stacks, two tall pillars of rock standing out from the sea, recalling the Welsh name for the hoards of guillemots which crown their tops in spring and summer. The nearby cliffs are nesting places for kittiwakes, razorbills, fulmars, petrels and shags. Finally, there is the Green Bridge of Wales, an incredible natural limestone arch jutting out from the cliff wall like the flying buttress of some stupendous cathedral. Beyond this, access is prohibited and one has to retrace one's steps or leave the cliffs and turn inland.

Pembroke Dock owes its development as a new town to the Admiralty when a dockyard was opened there in the early nineteenth century. An obelisk in the town centre records the names of the first two ships built and launched in 1816. In 1926 the dockyard was closed and for the next quarter of a century it became a base for Royal Air Force flying boats. The main feature of interest in the town is the large and plain classical Naval Chapel built in 1834, with a small tower and dome at one end. It now houses a motor museum including, amongst the assorted cars and motor bikes, an 1892 fire engine. In the dockyard there is also a Martello tower in good condition.

The upper part of the Milford Haven is known as the Daugleddau, a Welsh name meaning 'two swords', but a glance at the map shows a long winding channel eventually dividing into two branches which suggests more a Norwegian fjord, particularly as many of the names in this area are of Viking origin. Those expecting deep canyon-like rivers will be disappointed, however, for the Milford Haven and the Daugleddau are simply the remains of a valley system which was drowned by the sea when glaciers everywhere melted at the end of the Ice Age and the sea level rose. Instead of rocky mountains and cliffs the water is bordered by gentle hills clothed in fields and woods interspersed here and there with side-channels, inlets and salt marshes. Though undramatic, the great waterway, ever changing in direction and always interesting, is exceptionally attractive and unspoilt and has become, not surprisingly, a favourite resort for yachtsmen.

Neyland is the first town on the northern side of the Haven and is now accessible from the southern side by a fine new bridge. It owes its existence to Isambard Kingdom Brunel, who persuaded the South Wales Railway to make it their terminus in the west instead of Fishguard or Milford Haven. Brunel's plan was to make New Milford, as it was then known, a transatlantic port and it was even hoped at one time to sail the *Great Eastern* from there on her maiden voyage. But it was not to be and the new town became instead a terminal for the Irish steam packet until that trade too was taken over by Fishguard. A terrace of houses named after the *Great Eastern* still commemorates the hopes that were once cherished. The entrepreneurs of the period were not unduly put out, but made even more strenuous efforts to make New Milford the terminus of the proposed Manchester and Milford Railway. Parts of the new line, which would have given mid-Wales an alternative outlet for its flannel trade and Manchester an alternative port to Liverpool for importing raw cotton, were actually built near Aberystwyth and Llanidloes, but it was never completed and Neyland as a result never flourished as a great port.

'Milford Haven the most famous port in Christendom', wrote George Owen in 1603. Owen was referring to the haven itself for at that time only fields existed on the rising ground between Castle

Pill and Hubberston Pill where later the town was to be built. The town of Milford Haven is less than 200 years old and was planned almost from the start as a new town, with streets laid out to a gridiron pattern. Sir William Hamilton, the owner of the land, obtained an Act of Parliament in 1770 to establish a new town, but nothing was done until Sir William's nephew Charles Greville was appointed agent. Shortly before this time many Quaker whaling families were driven from Nantucket Island, Massachusetts, by the American War of Independence and had settled in Nova Scotia and France. Some of these were unhappy in their new homes and in 1793 Greville persuaded a few families to resettle in Milford Haven. From these small beginnings the new town developed.

The driving force behind the new town proposals was undoubtedly Greville, but it was the Quakers who made it alive. Between them they gradually got the embryo town on its feet, the Quakers setting up a whaling industry and surprisingly a brewery, while Greville persuaded the Admiralty to have some of its new warships built there. In 1797 Jean-Louis Barrallier, a French counter-revolutionary who had escaped from Toulon with the British fleet four years previously, was called in to plan the layout of the town. It is Barrallier's formal design based on three long parallel streets – Hamilton Terrace, Charles Street, and Robert Street – on a steeply rising hill above the harbour, which gives Milford its distinctive character today. Greville built the Custom House, an hotel, a quay and the rather stark St Katherine's Church. He also intended to establish a nautical college, but of this only an octagonal observatory was completed.

In the development of Milford Haven there were continual setbacks – the docks, for instance, were not completed until 1888 – and attempts were made to advertise the place as much as possible. On one occasion, in 1802, Nelson was invited to visit Milford to publicise its advantages. Unhesitatingly he praised the town in the most flattering terms and proclaimed the Haven, together with Trincomalee in Ceylon, as the finest natural harbour he had ever seen. Perhaps in extolling the virtues of Milford the naval hero was doing no more than fulfilling an obligation to his host Sir William Hamilton and his wife, for Lady Hamilton was none other than

Nelson's notorious mistress who before her marriage to Sir William had been Greville's mistress, Emma Hart.

On another occasion, in 1878, the *Great Eastern*, the largest ship in the world at that time, was brought to Milford for repairs, and while the publicity for the town was enormous the ship itself held up construction of the dock and was a source of acute embarrassment.

At one time Milford was the fourth most important fishing port in Britain, but the trade has gradually declined to the point of no return. Inshore fishing was the first to go on account of water pollution by oil tankers and it is the oil trade which is now the chief industry of both sides of the Haven. In a comparatively short space of time a number of vast oil terminals and refineries have sprung up and together with an enormous new power station they have, like the proverbial surveyor of Reading, 'completely altered her frontage'. Certainly in some instances well-known landscape architects have been consulted and attempts made to marry the new industries into the landscape, but such efforts are bound to be thwarted by the very scale of the enterprises themselves.

In two cases, nineteenth-century forts have been utilized to hide some of the oil company's work and this is a reminder that the oil installations were not the first trespassers on the Haven's landscape. The deep, safe waters of Milford Haven are ideal to oil tankers and navies alike. Indeed, it was reckoned to be big enough to hold the whole of the British navy at its largest and most powerful. It was from here that kings and armies sailed to the conquest of Ireland and it was here also that a French army landed to help Owain Glyndŵr in his hour of need and that 80 years later Henry VII landed with another French force to march to the defeat of Richard III. The fact that the Haven was so convenient to invaders, either going or coming, was a worrying thought throughout the centuries. To counter the possibility of invasion a couple of defensive blockhouses were built near the mouth of the Haven at Dale and Angle in the sixteenth century and a fort erected at Pill in the seventeenth century, but by the nineteenth century these had become obsolete.

The French Revolution coupled with the abortive French landing at Fishguard in 1797 renewed the fears of invasion and as a result an elaborate scheme for defending the Haven with forts, known as 'Palmerston's Follies', was drawn up and carried out during the middle years of the nineteenth century. Altogether in a period of little over twenty years, from 1840 onwards, fourteen forts, 'Martello' towers, blockhouses and batteries containing more than 200 guns were built along both sides of the Haven from its seaward entrance to as far back as Pembroke Dock. Most of the forts are now derelict but because of the indestructible way in which they were constructed they still form important landmarks along the banks of the Haven which remains a unique example of a defended port. Two of the forts stand near Dale at the northern entrance to the Haven. Dale Point Battery, built in 1856 and now a Field Studies Centre, was paired with a similar battery on Thorn Island (now a hotel) opposite. Likewise, the West Blockhouse Battery (built in 1857 and manned until as recently as 1950) on St Anne's Head was paired with the East Blockhouse Battery near Angle.

Dale village lies in a valley at the neck of the headland. Some of the houses huddle close to the curving shingle beach but the main part of the village consists of long parallel lines of houses on either side of the valley with a slim-towered church and a nineteenth century 'castle' at its head. A footpath at the end of the village leads to Westdale Bay with its dramatic cliff scenery and rock-strewn shore.

To the north is Marloes, a long straggling village once notorious for smugglers. The attraction of Marloes is its glorious beach – a great stretch of firm sand backed by superb rock and cliff scenery. The nearest road and car park is some distance away, however, and this prevents the beach becoming overcrowded. Gateholm Island, accessible by foot at low water and lying like a giant half-submerged whale, protects the sands from westerly winds. Virtually the whole of the flat top of the island is covered by an extremely large early Christian settlement (possibly of monastic origin) made up of long irregular chains of ruined stone huts grouped around courtyards. Since the island's rabbits became extinct some years ago, the shells of these huts have become very overgrown and are now difficult to make out on the ground.

A narrow, twisting lane from Marloes leads along the St Brides peninsula to Martin's Haven, a small but deep cove below the well-preserved earthworks of a promontory fort. From here, if the weather is fair, boats leave early in the morning for Skomer Island. This island was farmed until 1958, but now is run as a national nature reserve by the West Wales Naturalist Trust. The larger part of the island is accessible to visitors, but the peninsula known as the Neck (joined, incidentally to the main part of the island by a high and narrow isthmus only 12 yards wide) is used as a study area and is not open to the public. There is considerable evidence of Iron Age settlement on Skomer, but the chief interest must be the great colonies of seabirds nesting on the grey cliffs and the Atlantic seals which breed in the sea caves below the cliffs. The island also has its own special animal, the Skomer vole, a larger and tamer version of its mainland cousin. The red sandstone island of Skokholm two miles to the south has the oldest bird observatory in Britain. It was established by R. M. Lockley. He farmed the island for a dozen years and has described it in a number of his books.

CHAPTER TEN

Preseli

Haverfordwest (pronounced locally as Harford), or Hwlffordd in Welsh, lies almost exactly at the centre of the old county of Pembrokeshire. At one time it was the most important port in Wales for although six miles inland, the river on which it stands (Western Cleddau) at one time was navigable for cargo ships. The Custom House on the Old Quay still survives as one of the few reminders of the town's former nautical importance. Evidence of Haverfordwest's military history is more obvious. From the hill above the river the high curtain walls and circular tower of a Norman fortress glower formidably down over the shopping streets and dominate the whole town. In spite of the castle's fine strategic position and massive reconstruction in the thirteenth century it was not always easily held. As a bastion of the hated Norman advance and later as a centre of a strong Flemish community, Haverfordwest and its citadel remained a thorn in the flesh of the Welsh princes for many centuries. In 1136 Gruffydd ap Rhys captured the castle, in 1220 Llywelyn I burnt the town and in 1265 the castle was captured again. In 1405 Owain Glyndŵr, with the help of the French, sailed up the Milford Haven and captured the town but was unable to do more than besiege the castle. In 1648, after surrendering to the Parliamentary forces in the English Civil War, the castle was partly destroyed and it is a trifle disappointing to find, after a steep climb up from the main street, that as a result of the damage suffered then none of the interior buildings have survived. A gaol was erected within the castle ward in the nineteenth century and this has now been converted into a pleasant museum with delightful exhibits and displays.

Haverfordwest is full of interesting churches and chapels. St Martin's, at the rear of the castle, is the oldest and has an odd-looking leaning tower capped by a nineteenth-century spire. Nearby and hemmed in by roads and traffic at the top of High Street is St Mary's Church. Its cathedral-like interior is remarkably attractive. Above the tall clerestory windows of the nave there is an oak-panelled ceiling heavy with elaborately carved bosses and beams. The columns supporting the upper part of the nave have curious capitals amazingly carved with grotesque heads and animal figures; a monk holding an empty tankard upside down, a woman sticking her tongue out, a lamb biting a serpent, a pig playing a *crwth* (an old Welsh type of violin) and an ape playing a harp.

Just below St Mary's, on the corner of Dark Street and High Street, there is a red granite column marking the spot where William Nichol was burnt at the stake in 1558 for his religious views.

Of the chapels Bethesda Baptist (built 1878) and Tabernacle Congregational (built 1774 and restored 1874) are the best. Bethesda is built in Romanesque style with a large wheel window in the centre. Tabernacle has an unusual bow-fronted porch outside and a semi-circular apse inside. Of the old Augustinian Priory down by the river only fragmentary ruins remain.

Prendergast, once an independent village but now a suburb of Haverfordwest, lies on the east bank of the river and is of no especial interest except as the birthplace of George Stepney (1663-1707), statesman and poet. Stepney's politics varied with the monarch on the throne. At first under King James he was an ardent Tory and then when William and Anne ascended he determinedly embraced Whig principles and became, as a result, envoy to Poland and various German states. As for Stepney's verse, this only received faint approval from Dr Johnson who commented, 'in his original poems, now and then a happy line may perhaps be found, and now and then a short composition may give pleasure'. But then Johnson was never one to give praise freely.

The road north of Haverfordwest follows the Western Cleddau river towards Fishguard through a rocky gorge at Trefgarn. Here, where the river carves its way through an outlier of the Preseli hills, there are remains of ancient camps and earthworks hidden in the woods on either side of the valley. More dramatic and far older than these are the weirdly shaped outcrops on the western side. One, known as Poll Carn, resembles a sphinx and the other, known as Maiden Castle, looks like a monstrous ruined fortress, but both are the eroded remains of ancient volcanoes where the lava broke surface. The hard igneous rocks that resulted from the lava flows are now quarried for roadstone, but once there was supposed to have been a goldmine in the vicinity.

In medieval times the district had associations with both Owain Glyndŵr, whose mother owned the manor in the fourteenth century, and Henry VIII, whose ancestors were lords of Trefgarn. More recently, in the nineteenth century, Captain Jack Edwards bred the first Sealyham terriers at Sealyham Hall.

The gorge at Trefgarn marks the invisible boundary of the old county of Pembrokeshire into its Welsh and English parts. The land south of the gorge has been English in speech ever since it was settled by the Normans and later by the Flemings. The districts north of the gorge were also invaded by the Normans, but despite persistent pressure on their part they were never held permanently and to this day the language and culture of the area is primarily Welsh. Until recently the cultural boundary was a very tightly defined line known as the 'landsker', which had hardly changed over four centuries. So distinct was this boundary that it is said that a farmer on one side of it would be unable to converse with his neighbour on the other side. Since the Second World War the 'landsker' had begun to disintegrate, but unfortunately it is a one-sided development with the Welsh language on the losing side. Even so, most of the farm and place names north of Trefgarn are still Welsh, while nearly all the names south of the village are either English, Norman or Scandinavian. Similarly, the great majority of churches with Celtic type bell-cotes are north of the 'landsker', but the Norman type of church, with battlemented towers, is found mostly south of the boundary.

In medieval times a barren *rhos*, or no-man's-land lay along the margin of the 'landsker'. The tower of Roch Castle still stands silhouetted against the western sky at the seaward end of the *rhos* as

155

a reminder of the one-time existence of this wasteland and also as a reminder of the line of fortresses erected by the Normans to defend the territory won with difficulty from the Welsh princes of Dyfed. The castle was built by Adam de la Roche (Adam of the 'rhos') in the thirteenth century and after being in ruins for two centuries was converted into a private house at the beginning of this century.

It is difficult now to believe that in the late medieval period the Roch district was a centre of the West Dyfed coal industry. The coal was exported from nearby Nolton Haven, a wide gash in the edge of the land forming a delightful little bay surrounded by rocky cliffs which seem to slide down into the water. The haven faces south-westwards towards St Bride's Peninsula and Skomer Island so that the view out to sea appears like a large land-locked lagoon. Until the twentieth century coal mining was still an important industry here as can be seen from the ruins of the old Trefgarn Cliff Colliery (dating from about 1850) to the north of Nolton and from the iron rings and stanchions near the coast footpath which were used for mooring the sailing ships that carried the coal.

A long, curving, sandy beach stretches northwards as far as Newgale. At the furthest end of the beach there are traces of a submerged forest. In prehistoric times it covered the sands and the stumps of the old trees, worn down and polished into wooden stalagmites by the sea, are sometimes visible at very low tides after violent storms, such as occurred in 1172 when Giraldus Cambrensis passed this way. The whole coast is exposed to the Atlantic and in stormy weather pebbles are thrown up behind the beach, forming a great stony bank alongside the road. In one of these tremendous storms, in 1896, the inn by the side of the road was washed away and the landlady was only just able to rescue her daughter by hanging on to a branch of a tree. Luckily she also managed somehow to rescue £20 from the wreckage and with that she was able to build the present inn.

Beyond the stream at Newgale lies the holy cantref of Pebidiog (or Dewisland, as it is otherwise known). This land of Dewi, the most westerly promontory in Wales, was a famous haven of Christianity long centuries before the coming of the Normans. The Normans, as bloodthirsty and greedy as any other invaders, were also very devout and had a special reverence for religious sites as important as the home of Dewi Sant (St David). Thus Pebidiog was never the scene of any battles with the Normans and exceptionally in Wales no stone castle was ever built on this sacred wind-swept peninsula by either the Welsh princes or the Norman lords; this was the domain of the bishop of St David's and no troops were necessary to stand guard over the people, although the cathedral close was fortified just in case of trouble!

The landscape of the Pebidiog peninsula is one of the most distinctive and interesting in Wales. The rocks which form the basis of the scenery are amongst the oldest known to man and are extremely hard. In most places they are overlain by great thicknesses of younger rocks but here the ancient rocks come right to the surface. The soil cover is minimal, resulting in large expanses of badly drained ground and bare moorland, and here and there remnants of ancient volcanoes protrude ruggedly above the plateau. On the coast the sea has relentlessly eroded the rocks at every possible point of weakness. The coastal scenery is everywhere magnificent, with rocky cliffs up to 300 feet high deeply indented with numerous little inlets and bays.

One of the finest of the inlets is at Solva where the deeply etched river valley has been drowned by the sea to form a long narrow fjord-like harbour. The older part of the village, set back at the end of the harbour away from the sea, is picturesque with colour-washed cottages and opulent with swish sailing boats in summer. In winter it reverts to a more traditional Welsh atmosphere but its shipping trade and pirates have gone for ever, although occasionally debris brought up from the numerous shipwrecks just out to sea still stir the memory.

St David's, or more correctly Tyddewi (the House of Dewi), is the smallest city in Wales with a population of well under 2,000 inhabitants. The town overlooks Glyn Rhosyn (the Valley of Roses) where in the early sixth century Dewi Sant is reputed to have established his monastery just inland from the sea and out of sight of marauding sea raiders. Down the centuries all manner of people have taken the road to St David's in pious pilgrimage. In 1120 the Pope raised it to international status by making two journeys to Dewi's sanctuary equal to one to St Peter's in Rome and three journeys to Tyddewi equal to one to Jerusalem, the Holy City itself.

On entering the miniature town, however, one can be forgiven for wondering what all the fuss was about, for there is no sign of the great church that one has been led to expect. But go down the hill at the end of the street to the massive gateway known as Porth-y-twr and there in front of you is a spectacular view of the whole cathedral close laid out in splendid isolation in the hollow beside the Alun stream. The great cathedral, looking angular and austere but in keeping with its surroundings, stands in the centre of the close at the side of the stream; opposite is the ruined shell of the exotic Bishop's Palace and dotted around the enclosure are a number of chapels and various buildings concerned with the different functions of the cathedral.

St David is possibly the most popular of all the British patron saints, but strangely very little is known about him as a person and his life is shrouded in mystery. He is reputed to have been born about the year 520, the son of Non and a Ceredigion prince by the name of Sanctus (hence the name Dewi Sant). Most of his life was spent as leader of the monastic community which he had founded and he was well known for his strict discipline. As one of the great pioneers of Celtic Christianity in Britain during the period admiringly known as the 'Age of the Saints' Dewi was celebrated far and wide. In later centuries 50 churches were founded in southern Wales with his name. Giraldus Cambrensis was an ardent admirer of the saint and championed the autonomy of his church in the twelfth century when the Normans were trying to reorganise ecclesiastical administration in favour of the younger Canterbury Church. In Giraldus' words: 'The Bishopric of St David's became, as it were, a symbol of the independence of Wales ... and that is why David himself was exalted into a Patron Saint of Wales'. Dewi Sant is said to have died on the first day of March 588 and this day is now appropriately celebrated as the national day of Wales.

The cathedral that we see today – the last major church in Britain to be built in the Romanesque style of architecture – is the fourth church to occupy this historic spot. The first church was

apparently destroyed by fire in 645, as also was the second when it was plundered and burnt by Viking pillagers. The third church lasted until 1178, when the present building was started by Bishop Peter de Leia.

The interior of the cathedral is astonishing in every respect. The piers of the nave and the walls of the aisles lean visibly outwards and the fantastically decorated wooden ceiling, heavy with huge decorated oak pendants, seems ready to fall inwards, so that the whole building appears to be in imminent danger of collapse; add to this the extremely pronounced slope of the floor and the effect, especially if first seen on a stormy day, is disquieting to say the least. Yet though the building has in the past had its share of misfortune, such as the fall of the great central tower in 1220 and the Lady Chapel roof in 1775, it is safe enough today due to the massive buttresses added to the north wall and the curious internal flying buttresses below the aisle ceiling as well as the monumental restoration work carried out by Sir George Gilbert Scott in the latter part of the nineteenth century. After recovering from the initial surprise there is much to see in this magnificent building – truly the premier church in Wales – and it is worth spending some time in studying it and allowing a visit to the top of the tower to see the view. In contrast to the solid exterior the interior of the cathedral is elaborately ornamented and glows with the warm colour of mauve-pink stone. The unusually rich effect is not confined to the nave but continues through to the choir (with its beautiful rood-screen) and presbytery, culminating in an impressive group of lancet windows overlooking the Lady Chapel. Here below the lancet windows and behind the high altar the bones of Dewi Sant rest in a casket.

Parallel to the cathedral on the north side, what was once the cloister garth is the fourteenth-century College of St Mary, now converted into a cathedral hall. The Bishops's Palace facing the restored west front of the cathedral encloses three sides of a large court. The earliest part of the palace dates from the twelfth or thirteenth-century, but the most splendid part – the Great Hall – was built by Bishop Gower in the early fourteenth century. In its heyday it must have been a magnificent structure, though now it is merely an exotic ruined shell. A most attractive arcaded parapet veneered with a chequerwork pattern of multi-coloured stones and picturesquely edged in yellow moss runs along the upper part of the walls. The hollow interior of the Great Hall, lit at one end by a beautiful rose window, still has an air of pomp and splendour.

The Pebidiog peninsula abounds in history, particularly that concerned with the early Celtic Church. Immediately south of St David's are the remains of St Non's Chapel overlooking the sea. Named in honour of Dewi Sant's mother, it was built before the Norman invasion near the reputed birthplace of the patron saint. Nearby is a twentieth-century Roman Catholic chapel also dedicated to St Non and designed in imitation of a Celtic Chapel. From the winding path perched perilously above the cliffs south of the two chapels there are marvellous views of the rocks and creeks.

Porth Clais near the mouth of the Alun is the site of Capel y Pistyll (Chapel of the Spring) and traditional place of Dewi Sant's baptism. Further west at the foot of a deep cove are the remains of the Chapel of St Justinian, a friend of Dewi who suffered martyrdom on Ramsey Island just across the dark waters of the sound. Ramsey had two more ancient chapels and like Ynys Enlli in Gwynedd is reputedly the burial place of thousands of saints. Now the island, though looked after by the Royal Society for the Protection of Birds, is mostly occupied by rats and seals. Below the lifeboat slip at Porthstinan there are usually boats available for the journey to Ramsey or alternatively for a trip around the island.

Porth-Mawr, or Whitesands Bay, is associated with St Patrick, the patron saint of Ireland. This is traditionally the spot where he left Wales for the last time to go to Ireland. A plaque at the northern end of Traeth-mawr (the Great Beach) marks the site of his chapel. Here also is the supposed, but unlikely site of the Roman station of Menapia. From the top of rugged Carn Llidi overlooking the tip of the peninsula and Porth-mawr there is a splendid view (weather permitting) taking in the noble peaks of Eryri (Snowdonia) to the north and the Wicklow Hills of Ireland to the west. On the northern side of Carn Llidi there are remains of an Iron-Age promontory fort, a Stone-Age burial chamber and an ancient system of small irregular fields enclosed by rough stone walls. These fields were probably first farmed two thousand years ago and are thought to have been cultivated continuously since that time until the beginning of the present century.

From Carn Llidi to Fishguard the coastal scenery is superb. It is difficult and dangerous to get anywhere near the sea except through a few gaps in the almost unbroken chain of jagged cliffs. One of these favoured places is Abereiddi, where cars can park virtually by the seashore on one of the few beaches. At the end of the sands the gaunt jet-black shell of a slateworks building stands perched on a ridge. Beyond is a dramatic man-made lagoon carved out of the rocks. Originally a slate quarry, it was filled with water when the industry ceased and transformed into a crater-like harbour by blasting a channel to the sea. From 1850 to 1904 the quarry exported slates via a tramway across Ynys Barry, the departure point of St Barre (founder of Gouganebarra and Cork in Ireland), to Porth-gain a mile to the east. Here at Porth-gain a striking fjord-like inlet was artificially lengthened at one end to form a harbour for the slate ships. Overshadowing one side of the quarry is a macabre and derelict stone-crushing plant linked by tunnels to another deep quarry some way inland.

At Aberfelin and again at Abercastell the narrow coast road drops down briefly to sea level, passing on the way the ruined mill near Trefin that inspired the poet Crwys to write his famous poem *Melin Trefin*. Abercastell was a port in Tudor times but now relies on its fine sandy beach for the tourist trade. Between the two bays there is a massive Stone Age *cromlech* or burial chamber known, like a number of others in Wales, as Carreg Sampson.

Pen-caer is the big headland between Abercastell and Fishguard. On the western part of the headland the scenery is fierce and romantic erupting at Pwllderi in unfriendly cliffs that rise sheer out of the sea to the massive peak of Garn Fawr. A hill-fort with stone ramparts crowns the summit of Garn Fawr and here again there is a tremendous view embracing Cardigan Bay, the Preseli range and parts of northern Wales and Ireland. A memorial at the side of the cliff road halfway up Garn Fawr commemorates Dewi Emrys (1879-1952), a poet who wrote in the local dialect. A corbelled beehive type of hut in the yard of Tol Gaer farm nearby is said locally to be a prehistoric pigsty, but may in fact have been a Celtic hermitage. Another reminder of the district's association with early Christianity is Trefaser, the reputed birthplace in 707 of Bishop Asser, the friend and biographer of Alfred the Great.

Fishguard, the largest settlement between Haverfordwest and Aberystwyth lies scattered around the Gwaun estuary after which it gets its Welsh name Abergwaun. The town is really in three parts. The older part, known as Y Cwm or Lower Town, was once a fishing port and is now a charmingly attractive old-style village with variegated cottages strung out along one side of its harbour. Richard Fenton (1747-1821), poet and author of *A Historical Tour through Pembrokeshire*, lived at Plas Glynamel just outside the village.

Goodwick shelters on the west side of the bay beneath the Pen-caer headland. It also was a small fishing village until the beginning of this century, when it made a determined effort to become the premier terminal for Atlantic liners. Towards this end two great breakwaters were built and a fine new harbour opened in 1906. For a few years the port was used by the biggest and the best of the luxury liners, but with the outbreak of the First World War, the big ships stayed away and never came back. Now Goodwick is the terminal for the Irish ferry.

Upper Fishguard stands on the bulging hill between Y Cwm and Goodwick. Here is the shopping centre, the parish church and the 'Royal Oak', scene of the signing of the surrender of the last invasion of Britain. The invasion, or what at least was intended to be the catalyst that would stir up the local people into rebellion, took place at Carreg Wastad over the hill behind Goodwick in 1797. A force of between 1,200 and 1,400 French troops and convicts under the leadership of an Irish-American landed on the headland but after two days of looting they were rounded up, drunk with stolen liquor, by the Pembrokeshire Yeomanry on Goodwick Sands. More colourful, if unconfirmed, is the story of the surrender of the French invaders to Jemima Nicholas, a local lady cobbler, and her band of women. Dressed in traditional scarlet cloaks and tall hats and armed with pitchforks, the women marched to the top of the headland and were mistaken for red-coated soldiers by the French, who immediately lay down their arms and called for a truce. True or false, Jemima is reckoned to have captured a number of the invaders with her pitchfork and there is a memorial to her in St Mary's churchyard.

Beyond Fishguard the Pembroke Coast National Park widens inland to include Mynydd Preseli and the Gwaun valley. The sacred Mynydd Preseli is a desolate rolling moorland strewn with rocks and boulders. It forms the westernmost area of the Cambrian Mountains and, though only 1,750 feet above sea level at its highest point, has superb views over most of Dyfed and Cardigan Bay. Steeped in Welsh history and rich in prehistory, this was with Pebidiog once the hub of the Celtic world, standing at the crossroads of early routes between Wales, Ireland, southern England, the Scottish Hebrides and Brittany. Perhaps no other area in Wales has so many prehistoric antiquities. There are Stone Age burial chambers and standing stones, Bronze-Age round barrows, Early Iron Age hill-forts and hut circles. In addition, there are many Early Christian stones and crosses dating from the sixth to the eleventh century. Most of the remains are of religious significance and undoubtedly point to some special sanctity with which the mountains were thought to be endowed. It was here that the druidical temple-builders came some 4,000 years ago to collect the famous 'blue' stones for Stonehenge. More than 80 stones were quarried from the peak of Carn Meini at the eastern end of Preseli and then transported 200 miles over land by sledge and across the sea by raft to be erected eventually in the ritual circles on the Wiltshire Plain. Surprisingly, Mynydd Preseli has only one Stone-Age stone circle, near Mynachlog-ddu, and that a miniature compared to Stonehenge. On a less heroic note, it ought to be mentioned that in the last century slate was quarried near Mynachlog to roof the British Houses of Parliament in London.

The most famous of Preseli's ancient monuments is the Pentre Ifan *cromlech* near Carn Ingli. Pointed upright stones supporting a giant capstone 16 feet long make this a textbook example of its type, but the mound that once covered it has disappeared. Carn Ingli itself has a good example of a stone hillfort with hut circles. An even finer example, with three stone ramparts enclosing three large Bronze-Age burial mounds, covers the summit of Moel Drygarn near Crymych.

Mynydd Preseli has a hallowed place in Welsh folklore, being one of the main settings of that masterpiece of medieval European literature, the *Mabinogion*. Though the stories that comprise the saga were first written down in the Middle Ages, many of them are folk tales derived from a much earlier period, distant memories perhaps from the dawn of the Celtic world. Taken together they are a tantalising mixture of Celtic myths which attempt to give explanations to places and events. Intertwined with these themes are beginnings of Arthurian literature. In one story the Roman Emperor Magnus Maximus hunts in the forest of Y Freni Fawr near Crymych. Another story relates the meeting in the Cych valley of Pwyll, Prince of Dyfed, with the King of the Otherworld. In the story of Culhwch and Olwen love and courtship are mingled with the hunting of the Otherworld beast, Twrch Trwyth. Arthur of the Britons is called in to help Culhwch and the hunt starts at Porth Clais near St David's. The beast is then chased over Mynydd Preseli to Glyn Nyfer and across southern Wales to the Severn and eventually down to Cornwall, where it is driven into the sea. After the onerous task is completed Culhwch finally meets the chief giant Ysbaddaden and claims Olwen his daughter in marriage. The giant is killed and 'that night Culhwch slept with Olwen, and she was his only wife so long as he lived'.

Prehistory, history, legend and folk customs all seem to meet in this part of the world as though time has stood still. It is said that in the Gwaun Valley, for instance, New Year's Day is still celebrated in the middle of January in accordance with the Gregorian calendar, although the new calendar was introduced as long ago as 1752.

Even modern place names are derived from folklore, as in the case of Dinas Island, half way between Fishguard and Newport, which gets its name from a tale about fairies living in an underwater city (in Welsh, *dinas*). According to the legend, the fairies were much put out on one occasion when a fisherman dropped his anchor through the roof of their dwellings! Dinas Island, however, is not a true island, but a headland separated from the mainland by a flat-bottomed valley cutting across the neck of the promontory. The valley looks as though it might long ago have been a sea channel, but like the Gwaun valley, is in fact a remnant of the Ice Age when glaciers gouged their way across the land. Ynys Fach Llyffan Gawr, meaning 'Little Island of the Giant Llyfan', was the old Welsh name for the headland and was another attempt to explain this physical curiosity.

Newport stands at the northern base of Carn Ingli where the Afon Nyfer enters the sea. The Welsh name Trefdraeth 'town on the beach' is more appropriate for there are fine sandy stretches on both sides of the estuary. At one time it vied with Fishguard as the main port on this part of the coast. A stone castle dominated the town on the southern side and this gives a clue to its English name, for it was not always a port. When the Norman adventurer, Martin of Tours originally came to Preseli, he established his headquarters two miles upstream at Nevern and with the apparent acquiesence of the Welsh princes created for himself the virtually independent lordship of Cemais. As an added insurance the Norman baron married the daughter of the Lord Rhys, Prince of Deheubarth. Later William Martin inherited the new barony, but after quarrelling with his father-in-law was driven out of Castell Nanhyfer in 1191 and forthwith established a new castle and the 'new port' at the mouth of the river. Further attempts were made to drive the Normans and their half-Norman descendants out of the district by Llywelyn I in 1215, by Llywelyn II in 1257 and by Owain Glyndŵr at the beginning of the fifteenth century, but though Newport Castle was twice captured and once burnt the lordship survived right into the twentieth century. In 1857 the castle was partly restored and converted into a private residence.

Of the old castle at Nevern nothing remains except for some overgrown earthworks. The parish church has a history nearly twice as long as the castle and still stands, although in fairness it should be pointed out that the present rambling structure is a fifteenth-century rebuilding. It is said to have been founded in the sixth century by St Brynach and few sites have so much evidence of their early Christian history. Inside the church two ancient stones, one with Latin and Ogham inscriptions and the other carved with a cross, are used as window sills. A sixth-century pillar standing outside the porch commemorates, again in both Latin and Ogham, Vitalianus a Romano-British chieftain. The proudest possession, however, is the majestic tenth or eleventh-century Celtic cross that stands in the churchyard amongst gnarled yew trees. Both sides of the cross are subdivided into panels on which patterns of geometric and interlaced designs have been carved with superbly controlled skill. To complete the collection of ancient monuments there is a pilgrim's cross roughly carved on the bare rock on a hill to the west of the church. This has a kneeling recess below it and was probably used as a wayside shrine for travellers making their pilgrimage to St David's.

The most famous son of Nevern was George Owen (1552-1613), an antiquary and one of the Lords of Cemais. His chief claim to fame is the invaluable *Description of Pembrokeshire*, with its wealth of information not only about his own county but also about Wales generally. Owen recorded that wild deer were on the decrease in Preseli but the wild cattle, the 'Brocke, and such like wereof there is more store than is necessarye'.

One of the most interesting things in the *Description* is the account that Owen gives of a ferocious game called *cnapan*, a kind of rugby football played for hours on end between whole parishes. The *cnapan* itself was a wooden ball boiled in grease to make it slippery and the object of the game was to prevent the other side (or parish) from taking the ball back into their own territory. 'At some of these matches, there have often times been esteemed two thousand foote beside horsemen'. Mostly the *cnapan* was thrown, but occasionally the player would hold on to it and then Owen thought it 'a great thing to see a thousand naked men thus gripped together and beating one another over the head as hard as they be able'.

A century later the game appears to have been forgotten and the district reverted to more thoughtful ways. Religion once again became the overriding passion and Llwyngwair, a pleasant Georgian house halfway between Nevern and Newport, became the centre of non-conformism. Amongst the visitors to the house were John Wesley and William Williams Panycelyn, the famous Welsh hymn writer who is supposed to have composed many of his hymns there.

CHAPTER ELEVEN

Dyffryn Teifi
(The Teifi Valley)

The land to the west of the Afon Teifi is one of those cultural core areas of Wales which is distinguished more than anything by its apparent unchangeability. Changes do, of course occur, but they seem to take place more slowly here than elsewhere and one does not need to scratch deeply below the pastoral surface of the area to find remnants of a past way of life that have already disappeared from most other parts of Wales. The people are conservative to a degree in their habits; their cautiousness and shrewdness has made the name 'Cardi' synonomous in Wales with tight-fistedness. The grudging acceptance of change which is such a striking feature of inland Ceredigion generally and Dyffryn Teifi in particular makes it a latter-day explorer's paradise. Here one finds continuity with the past in the coracles and clay houses and rarities of nature such as the polecat. Dyffryn Teifi too is the main home of the Welsh wollen industry.

Symptomatic of the Welshness of the region is the revival of the old name Ceredigion for the district west of the Teifi. The Normans arrived first during the early twelfth century, but their influence was short lived. Under the leadership of Rhys ap Gruffydd the territory was won back to the royal house of Deheubarth in 1164. After driving out the Normans, Rhys (or the Lord Rhys as he was generally known), made his home in Cardigan, or Aberteifi, and rebuilt the castle there. One of the chief events for which Rhys is remembered is the first (or at least the earliest to be recorded) *eisteddfod*. It was held in Aberteifi castle during Christmas 1176 and appears to have been in every way a notable occasion. Though not then called an *eisteddfod* it had all the ingredients of the modern festival, including a national proclamation of the event twelve months in advance. Competitors were invited from England, Scotland and Ireland as well as from within Wales. A contemporary description in the remarkable chronicle *Brut y Tywysogion* recorded that 'the Lord Rhys held high festival in the castle of Aberteifi. He established two competitions, one for the bards and poets and another for the harpers and crowders and pipers and musicians of all kinds, with two chairs for the successful competitors, not to mention gifts of great value which he bestowed in addition'. Rhys was also a warm and generous patron of the Cistercian monasteries at Whitland and Ystrad Fflur. Nevertheless, when some twelve years after the first *eisteddfod*, the Archbishop of Canterbury visited Aberteifi on his famous pilgrimage through Wales to enlist volunteers for the Crusades Rhys was dissuaded by his wife from taking the cross.

The first stone castle, as opposed to the earliest castle of Rhys, at Aberteifi was not built until 1240 but little of this now remains, apart from remnants of a round keep, a drum tower incorporated in the fabric of a private house and part of the curtain wall. At the foot of the hill on which the castle ruins stand is a fine old six-arch bridge (built in 1726) crossing the Afon Teifi at the highest point to which ships could come. Tall warehouses on the opposite side of the river still give the place a nautical feel, but it is difficult now to realise that once Cardigan was one of the principal ports in Wales. From the foot of the hill Bridge Street winds upwards, past a furniture showroom which was once the eighteenth-century Shire Hall, and into narrow and bustling High Street, the commercial core of the town. At the end of High Street is the eye-catching Guildhall, a delightful Victorian-Gothic building put up in 1859, with multi-coloured pointed arches and a high roof. The clocktower was added in 1892. At the rear of the Guildhall is an arcaded market with a colourful basement full of busy stalls crowded between stout stone columns supporting low arches.

Few country towns in southern Wales have more of a Welsh personality (if one can use such a description for a town) than Cardigan. It is difficult, however, to put one's finger on the reason, especially as so much of the town dates from the nineteenth century. St Mary Street is the one street which has a pre-Victorian appearance and here in the Old Custom House, one finds a visual reminder of the town's earliest importance as a port. Another reminder of the past can be seen on the gravestones of eighteenth and nineteenth-century sailors in St Mary's Churchyard at the end of St Mary's Street. The church itself was largely rebuilt at the beginning of the eighteenth century, but the pinnacled chancel with its carved timber ceiling is original and dates from the fourteenth or fifteenth century.

At the rear of the church is the Priory, a house built in 1802 on the site of a twelfth-century Benedictine foundation. In front of the Priory wide lawns still sweep down to the riverside, but the house itself has been radically changed in character to suit its present purpose as a hospital and only the west front now bears much resemblance to John Nash's original design. It was here that Katherine Phillips, the poetess, lived until her early death at the age of 33 in 1664, from smallpox. Katherine was born in London, but came to live in Wales when she was 15 and at 17 she married James Phillips, the High Sheriff of Cardigan, who was then 54 years old and a widower. At her new home she created a kind of salon for her friends 'to discuss poetry and religion and the human heart'. Each friend was given a fanciful name, Katherine herself being known as 'Orinda'. She was highly regarded by contemporary poets, so much so that her death inspired a flood of eulogistic elegies, but now 'the incomparable Orinda', and her highly personal poems have been virtually forgotten.

St Dogmaels lies opposite Cardigan on the other side of the river. The most interesting thing here is the ruined abbey of St Mary the Virgin, a daughter house of the French abbey of Tiron. The abbey was founded before 1170 and completed 130 years later. Much of the church, including the Chapter House was rebuilt in the fourteenth century and enlarged by the addition of an elaborately vaulted north transept about 1500. Above ground only odd walls stand here and there, although the layout is easily visible, but below ground the vaulted crypt at the east end is still intact. The parish church was built in the mid-nineteenth century within the abbey grounds and has some Celtic inscribed stone crosses that are far older than the abbey. The ancientness of these stones suggest that originally this place was the sixth-century site of the Early Christian church of Llandudoch.

For dramatic architecture, one has to go three miles upstream to where the Teifi Valley becomes a gorge at Cilgerran. From the river the two great round towers of Cilgerran Castle look down from the cliff, making a splendid view that was recorded in paintings by both Richard Wilson (now in the National Museum of Wales) and J. M. W. Turner. The castle, in spite of its seemingly impregnable position, was captured on a number of occasions from its Norman builders, so that by the thirteenth century, it was in ruins. About 1240 the Normans set about building a new castle on the site, which is the one which has survived. In 1377 it was resurrected by the English king and subsequently occupied by the Vaughan family up to the seventeenth century, after which it fell once again into ruins.

Much of the large straggling village of Cilgerran, as well as the castle, is built of coarse grey-green slate which at one time was quarried locally. Except for a thirteenth-century tower the parish church is comparatively modern, having been built in the mid-nineteenth century (with dark stained-glass windows), but in the churchyard there is a sixth-century tombstone with Irish-type Ogham inscriptions commemorating the death of Trenugussus.

Older still is the *cwrgl*, or coracle, an ancient type of boat, which can still be seen on the Afon Teifi netting the sewin (sea-trout) and salmon which abound in the river. Almost circular in shape and propelled by a single paddle, the coracle is much the same now as it was in prehistoric times except that today tarred canvas is used over the flimsy structure of intertwined willow and hazel laths instead of animal skin. Light in weight, the coracle is carried on the back between one fishing stretch and another like a giant tortoise shell. The ideal time to see these craft in action is at the coracle race, which is held annually in August at Cilgerran. Unfortunately, the coracleman's way of netting fish is too efficient. New licences are no longer issued and thus, within a few years coracle fishing may well be a thing of the past.

A few miles upstream is Cenarth, another excellent place to see coracles. This is the highest point to which the coracle can be paddled. The surroundings are exceptionally attractive. An elegant two-arch bridge (with circular flood holes) leaps across the swirling river and frames a fine view of water cascading over rocks in the background.

As well as being one of the last homes of the coracle, the Teifi is known to be the last resort of the beaver in Wales. The first written mention of beavers in Britain was in the laws of Hywel Dda, which decreed that the king was to have the worth of any beavers wherever found. In Hywel's time the beaver was already rare and its skin was consequently five times the value of a marten's and ten times more valuable than the skin of any other animal. Giraldus Cambrensis in his *Description of Wales* also refers to the beaver being found in the Teifi, but nowhere else in England or Wales. By the beginning of the sixteenth century the beaver had probably disappeared from Dyffryn Teifi as well.

Mention of Giraldus is a reminder that the castle of Cenarth Bychan, its exact site unknown but somewhere in this district, was the home for a time of the glamorous Nest, the Welsh 'Helen of Troy'. Her story is colourful, though it did little to help the fortunes of the Welsh. She was born the daughter of Rhys ap Tewdwr, the last king of an independent Deheubarth which at that time extended over the whole of southern Wales except for parts of Glamorgan and Gwent. Her attractions must have been irresistible for there was no shortage of willing suitors for her hand. But although she herself seems not to have been seriously upset by the affairs of love she certainly upset the King of England and created havoc among the Welsh princes so that they were unwilling to unite and thus put paid to any hope of stemming the Norman advance into western Wales.

Henry I was the first to fall for the princess and, with not the most honourable of intentions, he made Nest his ward after her father's death in 1093; from this somewhat dubious alliance sprang the family of Fitz Henry. Having tired of Nest and anxious to marry the Scottish King's daughter Henry then had the Welsh princess married to his Constable at Pembroke, Gerald de Windsor; from this union sprang the family of Fitz Gerald and Angharad, the mother of Giraldus Cambrensis. The de Windsors lived together at Cenarth Bychan and while here Nest met her cousin Owain, the dashing and reckless son of Cadwgan, Prince of Powys and Ceredigion. Having once fallen under Nest's spell Owain lost no time. He raided the castle during Christmas 1109 and carried her off, perhaps not unwillingly, to his father's estate near Llangollen in the north. With this amorous act, all hell was let loose. Henry I invaded and devastated Ceredigion, giving the princedom to a Norman bootlegger, and thus ending Welsh rule for more than a quarter of a century. Cadwgan was to weak to resist the unleashed might of England and Owain sought refuge in an Irish boat moored in the Dyfi estuary and escaped across the sea. Owain later returned to Wales but was killed in battle in Dyffryn Tywi, ironically, almost by accident at the hand of Nest's lawful husband Gerald de Windsor, while fighting to defend his heritage and territorial rights. Eventually, after Gerald died, Nest decided to marry again. This time she married a prince of her own race Gruffydd ap Rhys, the result of which was yet another great family line.

Immediately east of the Cenarth gorge the scene is more placid, with the Teifi winding along the flat valley bottom in a series of loops until at Castell Newydd (Newcastle Emlyn) it doubles back on itself twice to form two attenuated peninsulas. On one of these narrow strands the 'new castle' was built in the thirteenth century by Prince Maredudd ap Rhys of Dinefwr to replace an older one on the opposite bank. The present fragmentary remains, however, belong to a fifteenth-century fortified mansion built by Sir Rhys ap Thomas. It played its part in the English Civil War by being the last castle in southern Wales to hold out for the king and then after succumbing, it was ignominiously demolished.

Castell Newydd was founded as a borough in 1303 and for a long time was twinned by the episcopal borough of Adpar on the opposite side of the Teifi. A castle mound at Adpar belonged to the Bishop of St David and by 1326 the borough itself had 96 burgages, presumably on the flat terrace land west of the bridge. The borough was dissolved in 1741 and now the site is featureless. Adpar is of interest, however, as the site of the first printing press in Wales, set up in 1718 by one Isaac Carter in the house by the bridge.

In the eighteenth and nineteenth centuries Ceredigion was regarded as being agriculturally one of the poorest counties in Wales. Naturally, even in this region some parts were better than others and one of the most fertile areas was the district between Castell Newydd and Lampeter. It was here that many of the larger houses were built. Few, however, were really large compared with mansions found in other parts of the country and a Gothic house like Bronwydd, a few miles north of the river, was exceptional. Bronwydd was built in 1855 but is now a sad and forlorn ruin. It is best seen today from a distance – then the tall Grimm's fairy-tale-type towers and turrets are romantically outlined in silhouette. Nearer, the decrepit ruins are pathetic reminders of a past glory and the still clear inscriptions on all the doorways, such as 'Home Sweet Home' seem bitterly ironic.

Llandysul is today the main centre of the Welsh woollen industry. Within a small radius of this pleasantly situated village there are no less than six woollen mills in most of which visitors can actually see the weaving being carried out. The woollen industry grew up in isolated farmsteads in which handlooms were used, before it developed into a sizeable industry scattered over the countryside. In northern Wales, especially in the Severn Valley, many large factory mills were established in the nineteenth century, but these have all closed and the industry is now concentrated almost entirely in Dyffryn Teifi. The mills are driven by water power and usually sited on fast-flowing tributary streams such as the Ceri, Cletwr and Bargod. The heyday of the local woollen industry was in the late nineteenth century when the mills were fully occupied in making woollen shirts for miners in the southern coalfield. Nowadays the mills produce flannels, tweeds, tapestries and most importantly, bedcovers using both traditional and modern designs. The traditional Welsh bedcover known as a *carthen* has become deservedly popular both as an attractively designed bedspread (or even as a lightweight carpet) in the daytime or as a warm blanket at night.

Llandysul was also the birthplace of the one-eyed preacher

Christmas Evans. In a land renowned for its preachers, none was better known and loved than this one. During the golden age of Welsh preaching he was one of its most outstanding orators and was considered to be unequalled for his imaginative descriptions. In the words of the poet Hiraethog, 'Evans was aglow throughout, like the volcano Etna or Vesuvius, casting out his lava like a seething river over his listeners until the emotions were aroused'. Contemporary paintings of the preacher with his one 'large and protruding eye' depicted him as an awe-inspiring person and yet he was 17 before he could read at all. He was born in a small cottage near Llandysul and started work as a parish apprentice on various farms in the locality before moving north to Gwynedd as an itinerant preacher at the age of 22. He died in Swansea in 1838. Christmas Evans was a master of *hwyl*, an art whereby the preacher works himself into a passionate frenzy and utters his sentences in a high-pitched sing-song voice to stir up the emotions of his congregation. *Hwyl*, however, means much more than hysterics – it is one of those Welsh words of which there is no adequate English equivalent, yet it is understood throughout Wales by Welsh speakers and non-Welsh speakers alike. It can mean religious fervour or humour, but more than anything, it means doing something with real feeling. In Wales this often has a religious connotation. A good example is the famous but short-lived Evan Roberts Revival at the beginning of the present century. This religious revival started at the small village of Blaenannerch near Cardigan on 29 September 1904. Although Evan Roberts was the centre of attraction at the special services held all over Wales during the ensuing months, it was the tremendous enthusiasm or *hwyl* of the congregations and not the minister that made these services such momentous events, for Roberts himself had comparatively little to say.

Llanybydder on the eastern banks of the Teifi is a pleasant but architecturally unremarkable market village straggling out in four directions from the main road crossing. Its claim to fame is its monthly horsefair, held in the Mart next to the churchyard. The fair, held on the last Thursday of every month, is still a sizeable one in spite of the motor car and is in fact the largest of its kind in

Wales, if not Britain.

The next place of any consequence going up the Teifi Valley is Lampeter, or more correctly in Welsh, Llanbedr-pont-Steffan. It was established as a borough between 1271 and 1277, but even before this time it must have been an important crossing place of the Teifi, for there was certainly a bridge (the original Pont Steffan) here in the twelfth century. The present bridge, however, dates from 1933 when it was rebuilt after disastrous floods. The borough would have been centred on the old castle, the mound of which still survives in the grounds of St David's College. Bishop Burgess of St David's founded the College in 1822, but although the emphasis has always been on training for holy orders, it has never been solely a theological college. It was originally affiliated to the Universities of Oxford and Cambridge and thus when the pro-nonconformist University of Wales was founded in 1893, St David's remained outside the orbit of the national university because of religious and political prejudices. In 1970 a new charter reversed the traditional role of St David's and it became a constituent college of the Welsh university. The old Oxbridge affiliation is reflected in the architecture of the original college building, designed by C. R. Cockerell in a rather weakly detailed Perpendicular Gothic style as a two-storey quadrangular block. The entrance, through an arched gateway on the south side, leads to an internal courtyard and a cloistered north wing containing the old library and chapel. The modern buildings erected in the college grounds since 1963 are generally restrained in character and fit inoffensively with the older buildings. In one of the new halls of residence a cloistered arcade with pointed arches has been incorporated into the design in order to help the new merge with the old.

On the whole the town of Lampeter seems to have had a peaceful existence and has not been directly involved in any wars or rebellions since its castle was destroyed by Owain Gwynedd as far back as 1137. One event, from the beginning of the seventeenth century, concerning the mansion of Maes-y-felin does, however, stand out. The daughter of the house was once found in compromising circumstances with the son of Vicar Prichard of Llandovery, and following this the Vicar's son was hounded by the girls' brothers and eventually murdered. In return, Vicar Prichard swore a curse on Maes-y-felin. The curse was apparently an effective one, for later the house was burnt to the ground. Its stones were used to build a new house at Peterwell in the eighteenth century for the infamous Sir Herbert Lloyd, but that house too was destroyed by fire and is now marked by nothing more than some ruined walls.

A detour west of Lampeter brings one to the Afon Aeron flowing down through a broad flat-bottomed vale to Aberaeron and the sea. Aberaeron is reputed to have been planned by John Nash and though there is no written evidence to support this claim it is obvious from the orderly street pattern that the layout of this attractive port was the work of one man. The development of Aberaeron as a new town dates from the early years of the nineteenth century and at this period Nash was engaged in designing some country houses in the neighbourhood. Certainly the general character of some of the terraces, modest though they are, suggest that they might well have been designed in Nash's office at Carmarthen, though Nash himself had by then returned to work in London. The plan of Aberaeron is loosely based on two large open-ended squares, one enclosing a large playing-field and the other, on the opposite side of the main road, partially enclosing the harbour, which was constructed between 1807 and 1811. Like most of the new ports on the west coast, Aberaeron was largely the result of a local enthusiast who wished to develop his estates and make it into an outlet serving the surrounding countryside. In this case it was the brainchild of the Rev. Alban Gwynne after he had inherited the local Mynachty estate.

At one time Aberaeron had three small shipbuilding yards and steamships continued to use the harbour until 1934. With the coming of the railway in 1911, however, shipping went into decline. The railway itself was closed to passenger traffic 40 years later and now the town is a quiet holiday and administrative centre.

New Quay, or Cei Newydd, a few miles south is a complete contrast. Both places are roughly the same size, but just as Aberaeron is almost as flat as a pancake, New Quay is a steep and hilly headland, and whereas one has rectilinear streets with terraces all of the same size, the other has winding lanes and houses jumbled up together. New Quay also has delightful curving bays with sandy beaches and a quaint solid-stone quay and slipway. Parking near the beach, however, is almost impossible unless one arrives early.

The road back from Aberaeron to Tregaron and Dyffryn Teifi passes close to Llyn Eiddwen set high up in the most desolate part of Mynydd Bach. The little lake, which is also the source of the Afon Aeron, has a romantic atmosphere despite the bleak appearance of the surrounding countryside. It is at its most appealing in the evening twilight, when one can imagine with little difficulty the 'castle' that once stood on the island at the southern end of the lake. The 'castle' was built by a Mr Treadwell as his country house while he went prospecting for lead in the vicinity. He found no lead, however, and with his hopes and fortunes unrealised he abandoned the toy fortress on the island to the elements.

A few miles down the Aeron valley is Llangeithio, a tranquil village which was once the stamping ground of the Rev. Daniel Rowlands, one of Wales' greatest preachers. With colleagues such as Griffith Jones of Llanddowror and Hywel Harries of Trefeca, Rowlands helped to fan the flame of Methodism throughout the country in the eighteenth century. In 1763 he was suspended from clerical duties for his over-enthusiasm, but undaunted he built his own chapel at Llangeithio to accommodate the crowds who came to listen to him. Reputedly up to 3,000 people came to Llangeithio on occasions to hear the great preacher; they arrived in flocks from all parts of Wales, tramping over what were then almost non-existent roads – such was the power of his terrifying and fiery sermons.

Llanddewibrefi, just to the south of Tregaron, is an attractive village abounding in history. Opposite the village by the Teifi is Pontllanio, the site of a Roman fort. No vestige of the fort now remains above ground, but a Roman bath-house was excavated there in 1887 and fine Roman inscribed stones have been found on the site. The fort stood on the line of a Roman road traditionally known in Welsh as Sarn Helen after the Welsh wife of the usurper emperor Magnus Maximus. In early Christian times

Llanddewibrefi must have been an important centre of the Celtic church. It was here, in the early sixth century, that Dewi Sant (St David) is supposed to have addressed a famous meeting called to enforce stricter discipline within the church. The tradition that while Dewi Sant was speaking the ground rose up to form a plat-form (hence the mound on which the present church stands) can be safely ignored. With the famous Idnert Stone, recording the murder of the abbot of Llanbadarn Fawr, we are on safer ground for this is also the first written reference we have to Wales' patron saint. The stone, dating from the sixth century, was discovered in 1698 by Edward Lhuyd but subsequently, during repairs to the church, it was broken up a stonemason and rebuilt into the outer wall of the tower. Two pieces of the stone (one part upside down) can be seen today and the inscription is still legible after 1,400 years. The massive twelfth-century tower is now the oldest part of the church, although of course, there must have been a church here long before. The original medieval church had two large transepts, but these fell down in the early nineteenth century and the arches of the transept can now be seen outlined on the face of the tower. In spite of this considerable loss and the virtual rebuilding of the nave and chancel in the late nineteenth century the church is still a noble building. Its early association with the Celtic church is recorded inside by three ancient inscribed stones (one with Ogham writing) and by a modern statue of Dewi Sant. Another record, now kept outside Wales in the Bodleian Library at Oxford, is *Llyfr Ancr Llanddewi Brefi*, a famous manuscript written at Llanddewi in 1346 containing among other things the earliest Welsh translation of Rhigyfarch's *Life of St David*.

The ancient market town of Tregaron is thoroughly Welsh in every way, and seems to have changed but little over the years. Its peacefulness makes an appropriate setting for the bronze statue of Henry Richard. Henry Richard was born in Tregaron in 1812 and became known as the 'Apostle of Peace' for his pioneering advocacy of international arbitration as a method of settling disputes. International peace was, however, only one of the interests of this Congregational Minister and member of Parliament. He was involved in the new spirit of nationalism that grew up in Wales during the latter part of the nineteenth century and protested strongly against the local landlords who had evicted their tenants because of their religious and political views. Partly as a result of Richard's opposition to the landlords' oppressive methods, the Ballot Act of 1872 was passed.

Another Tregaron hero was Thomas Jones, better known as the Twm Sion Catti, the sixteenth-century outlaw who haunted the upper reaches of Dyffryn Tywi north of Llandovery.

The most famous feature of the Tregaron district is the great peat bog known as Cors Goch Glanteifi (The Red Bog beside the Teifi), its name being derived from the rich red colouring of the cotton sedges when they die in autumn. In summer the white fruit of the cotton sedge transforms the bog into a snow-like carpet. Ten thousand years ago Cors Goch was a large shallow lake formed towards the end of the Great Ice Age by melting glaciers. Eventually the lake drained and became bog. Now it is a national nature reserve and access is allowed to permit holders only. With a permit one can walk for five miles alongside the Teifi through the centre of the bog, but after periods of heavy rain the possibility of sudden flooding can make such a walk dangerous. The bog is relatively useless for agriculture, and apart from some peat cutting around the edges it has been largely undisturbed by humans. Consequently, it is rich in wild life, particularly birds. Seventy species of birds breed regularly on or around the bog. In winter hundreds of white-fronted geese come every year from Greenland. Winter is also the time to see whooper swans and hen harriers, and occasionally kites and merlins. In addition, the bog is one of the few homes of the rare large heath butterfly.

The flowers that carpet Cors Goch in the spring may well have given raise to the name of the nearby Cistercian abbey of Ystrad Fflur. Both in Welsh and Latin (Strata Florida), the name means 'flowery levels'. Here, between 1184 and 1235, the most Welsh of Welsh abbeys was built under the patronage of the Lord Rhys. The ravages of despoilers and the weather have reduced it to fragmentary ruins. Enough remains, however, to show that architecturally it had some unusual features, such as the continuous stone screen walls which divided the spaces between the piers separating the nave from the aisles. More significant is the great west doorway with its unique semi-circular arch. Around the arch are six bands of roll mouldings, the outer one of which ends in a spiral scroll incorporating a three-legged emblem known as a triskel. This triskel was a favourite motif in Celtic art of the Early Iron Age and its appearance at Ystrad Fflur shows how great has been the continuity of some traditions in Wales. In fact the tradition of native craftsmanship must have been very strong indeed, for normally the Cistercian monks were opposed to any kind of ostentatious decoration.

In other ways the Cistercians had a beneficial influence. Large areas of land in mid-Wales were owned by the monks of Ystrad Fflur; sheep were introduced and the monks developed the woollen industry of Ceredigion to such an extent that they were given a royal licence by King John to sell and export wool. The monks also established a fair at Ffair-rhos (now held at Pontrhydfendigaid) and stocked the desolate Teifi pools with trout for the first time. Ystrad Fflur itself became an important centre of Welsh culture and learning. The famous *Brut y Tywysogion* (Chronicle of the Princes), with its wealth of information about Wales in the Middle Ages, was largely written here by the Cistercian monks. An equally famous possession in medieval times was the *Cwpan* (The Holy Grail of Arthurian legend), a wooden cup with healing powers reputedly carved from the Cross. With the Dissolution of the abbey the *Cwpan* was taken to Nanteos near Aberystwyth.

By the thirteenth century Ystrad Fflur had become the national sanctuary and during that century no less than nine of the minor Welsh princes were buried there. Better known than most of these, however, is Dafydd ap Gwilym, the great fourteenth-century Welsh poet who according to tradition was buried under the yew tree at the side of the abbey. Dafydd's poems were inspired as much by the work of French troubadours as by the subtle metrical forms of traditional Welsh poetry. He enlarged the scope of Welsh poetry, simplified its language and perfected a new type of poem known as the *cywydd*. His poems came as a lyrical breath of fresh air blowing away the archaic cobwebs, and like the troubadours' songs had themes based on love and nature. But whereas the troubadours sang of romantic love, Dafydd's beautiful love poems were of a much more erotic kind. Personal descriptions, however, are generally vague in Dafydd's poems, for the poet was always in a hurry to get his girl to the woods. In the nature poems, on the other hand, the poet described the birds and beasts and seasons in a great detail based on his own observations. This was not only something new to Welsh poetry, but was almost without precedent in European literature. His descriptions take various forms, but most notably by comparison with other features. In this art of multiple similitude, known in Welsh as *dyfalu*, Dafydd ap Gwilym was the greatest master of them all. Here, for example, is the way in which he compares a mist that prevented him from meeting one of his girlfriends,

> *A cloak from the grey-black sky,*
> *a very endless coverlet,*
> *a blanket of distant heavy rain,*
> *black weaving from far, hides the world,*
> *an exhalation from the far oven of hell,*
> *the smoke of the world from a far source,*
> *goblin-fire smoke from the underworld,*
> *a thick habit for this world,*
> *a lofty weaving of spiders*
> *filling each place like a sea.* *

Even in the English translation it is a memorable description, but in Welsh it is magical. But it is more than just a good poem, it is distinctly Welsh in spirit.

It has no central climax, as in poetry belonging to the Continental tradition, but instead has an even tracery of subtly-woven epithets which evoke the mood of Celtic interlaced sculpture or the intricate carving of a late medieval roodscreen.

Dafydd ap Gwilym's love of the countryside was a means of retreat from the Englishness of the new order imposed on Welsh life after the death of Llywelyn Fawr in 1282. He made no explicit protest against the alien government but instead raised Welsh poetry to new heights. In this way he is just as much a hero of the

* Gwyn Williams: *An Introduction to Welsh Poetry*

183

Welsh nation as Owain Glyndŵr was to be a few years later and it is entirely appropriate, therefore, that he should have been laid to rest in the sanctuary of Ystrad Fflur.

CHAPTER TWELVE

Aberystwyth And Pumlumon

The scenery of northern Ceredigion is rugged and dramatic compared to the southern part of the old county. The difference is due largely to the way in which the river system has developed.

A million or more years ago, before the Great Ice Age changed the face of the country the source of the Afon Teifi was on the western slopes of Pumlumon. Then, as a result of erosion, the upper course of the Teifi was 'captured' by younger streams running westwards and diverted into the Ystwyth and Rheidol rivers. Geologists recognise the present sudden sharp bends in the Afon Ystwyth at Pont-rhyd-y-groes and the Afon Rheidol at Pontarfynach (Devil's Bridge) as being the points where the older Teifi was intercepted by the fast-flowing young rivers. Two remarkable wind gaps, or dry valleys, between Pontrhydfendigaid, Pont-rhyd-y-groes and Pontarfynach provide further evidence of the ancient course of the Teifi.

At Ysbyty Ystwyth there is a spacious Victorian church (1879) nobly sited on the hill above the village and the original but now derelict parish church. From the 'new' church there are some magnificent views across to the heavily wooded Ystwyth valley a hundred yards below and of the little village of Pont-rhyd-y-groes perched on a narrow shelf above the river. In the nineteenth century Pont-rhyd-y-groes was a prosperous mining settlement. In fact it was the centre of the most important lead mining area in Wales. Fortunately, although remains of lead workings can still be seen at many places in the vicinity, the industry had little effect on the picturesque appearance of the village.

One of the more attractive features left behind from the abandoned leadmines are the numerous reservoirs dotted around the hills in this part of Ceredigion. Some of these reservoirs, such as the six constructed for the Fron-goch and Wemyss leadmines to the north-west of Pont-rhyd-y-groes, are quite large. In this case, each reservoir was connected by artificial streams to work 15 water-wheels, varying in diameter from 12 feet to a giant 55 feet. Production at the mines ceased at the beginning of the present century and now all that remains is a complex of ruined stone buildings, aqueducts, tramways and shafts. The remains of another large leadmine can be seen at Cwmystwyth alongside the mountain road to the Elan valley and Rhaeadr. Here the old tips and quarries scattered on the hillsides, together with rusting remains of a large concentrating mill (used for separating the lead out of the worthless rock) lend an eerie and desolate appearance to the place, almost as though one had suddenly come upon a ghost town. The Cwmystwyth mine was one of the oldest in mid-Wales, having been worked on and off for many centuries. Originally charcoal was used to smelt the lead ore locally, but so much wood was used in this way to make the charcoal that even by the early sixteenth century the valley had become almost bare of trees.

The heyday of lead mining in Ceredigion was the middle part of the nineteenth century when the metal was in great demand for the ever-growing towns and new industries. At one time or another during that period there were more than 90 leadmines in the northern half of Ceredigion, but as the price of lead fell in the latter part of the nineteenth century, due to competition from abroad, the industry declined. The Cwmystwyth mine had something of a revival at the beginning of this century during which time silver was also extracted, but in 1916 the mine closed for good.

More than a century earlier the Ystwyth valley had been the scene of an unusual venture by Thomas Johnes to improve the district and provide work for the people who lived there. One of the few reminders now of this experiment is the eighteenth-century bridge near the end of the valley at Blaen-y-cwm. This was built by the Bath architect, Thomas Baldwin for Johnes to provide a better access from the east to his romantic country mansion of Hafod

Uchtryd. Though Hafod Uchtryd itself has been demolished and the site is occupied by caravans the story of the house is worth mentioning – it is one of trial and error in the face of great difficulties and of good intentions transmuted to poignant sadness.

When Thomas Johnes inherited Hafod (the name means 'summer dwelling'), from his father it was the lonely and run-down centre of a 'beggarly estate', which could only be reached by a difficult and sometimes dangerous journey across wild open mountains and unbridged torrents. The surroundings, despite their naturally dramatic beauty, had been stripped bare of trees and were uninviting to the average eighteenth-century gentleman. The area was almost completely unknown to English travellers and was largely peopled by wretched miners and impoverished peasants, many of whom lived in clay cottages which were little more than mud hovels – the landlords being generally absentees. The Johnes family hailed originally from Llanfair Clydogau, near Lampeter, but Thomas himself was brought up at Croft Castle on the Hereford border amongst the wealthy Knight family. At Croft Castle Thomas, and his cousin Richard Payne Knight, together with Uvedale Price, formed a group of enlightened country gentlemen who advocated the Picturesque cult, a theory which attempted to merge informal landscape gardening with romantic architecture to make a naturalistic whole.

In the autumn of 1783 Johnes turned his back on Croft Castle and went to live at Hafod to spend the rest of his active life transforming the house and its surroundings into 'Elysium' in accordance with his Picturesque ideals. Within a few years he had planted acres of young trees across the mountain sides, opened up views of the natural waterfalls and grottoes to reveal their beauty, constructed roads and drives through the estate and built bridges. In 1786 the foundation stone for a large new Gothic mansion with embattled parapets and weird pinnacles was laid by Jane Johnes of Dolaucothi, whom Thomas had secretly married in 1784. The architect for the new Hafod was Thomas Baldwin, but Johnes himself appears to have been the designer of the oriental-looking octagonal library which was immediately proclaimed as 'the triumph of the place'. Coleridge saw the Moorish dome amongst its romantic surroundings when he passed that way on a tour of Wales and it may well have been this extraordinary piece of architecture that gave the poet the idea that eventually blossomed into the stately pleasure dome of Kubla Khan...

> *And there were gardens bright with sinuous rills*
> *Where blossomed many an incense-burning tree;*
> *And here were forests ancient as the hills,*
> *Enfolding sunny spots of greenery.*

Luxuriant gardens abounded in the precincts of the house. There was a special flower garden, entered through a gateway carved with figures of Adam and Eve, in the woods above the river for Jane Johnes. Behind this, on a rocky summit and reached by a series of zig-zag paths, was an even more special flower garden for Mariamne, Johnes' crippled daughter. It was here, at the top of the path, that an obelisk was erected to commemorate the Duke of Bedford.

For a while Hafod was indeed a place of ideal happiness, but in 1807 the first tragedy struck. The house, with its priceless collection of Welsh and French manuscripts was destroyed by a fire which started in the attic and quickly spread. Frozen springs and wells did not help in fighting the blaze. 'Stunned but not knocked down', Johnes got Baldwin to rebuild the house as before.

In 1811 there was a second tragedy when Johnes' beloved daughter Mariamne died at the age of 27, after a few days illness. From this blow Johnes never recovered and within two years of Mariamne's death, he left Hafod and retired to Devon. Hafod was sold and then gradually deteriorated, although as late as 1854, George Borrow was able to describe it as 'a truly fairy place ... beautiful but fantastic'. In 1932, Eglwys Newydd, the new church which Johnes had had Wyatt to design on the estate, was destroyed by fire and with it the monument of Mariamne by Chantrey. In 1950, the crumbling mansion itself was blown up; all that remains of Hafod is the Duke of Bedford's column and Mariamne's flower garden pathetically overgrown now but still revealing through the trees a magnificent view down the Ystwyth valley of forests, mountains and tumbling streams. Here one can still recapture something of the spirit of Johnes' Xanadu in 'that romantic chasm' where 'with a mazy motion through wood and dale the sacred river ran'.

West of Pont-rhyd-y-groes the road follows the Ystwyth in a trench-like valley between looming forest-clad mountains as far as Llanafon and Trawsgoed.

Llanafon is a small straggling village that seems to creep up the adjoining valley into the depths of the forest. The church (rebuilt 1860) at the lower end of the village is dark and gloomy inside, with late nineteenth-century stained-glass windows, mostly dedicated to members of the Lisburne family.

The Lisburne crest and motto also adorns the pediment of nearby Trawsgoed, the headquarters of the National Agricultural Advisory Service. The main façade, with its Ionic porch, dates from the late eighteenth century, but the rest of the house was rebuilt in the nineteenth century in the style of a French château. Inside, there is an exotic library elaborately decorated with panelled ceilings and fluted columns, while outside there are attractive formal gardens and a fine avenue of conifers.

The valleys open out after Trawsgoed and the road leaves the wide flood plain of the Ystwyth to take a short cut over the ridge to the mouth of the river at Aberystwyth. On the way the road passes close to two places of somewhat exceptional interest. The first is the stately but austere Palladian-style mansion of Nanteos nestling in a small rounded *cwm* near the source of Nant Paith and overlooking a rolling landscape of parkland and hills. Three storeys high and almost square on plan, the mansion was built in 1739 and added to at a later date. Architecturally, the most noteworthy feature of the place is the Greek Revival entrance screen to the stable block at the rear of the house. The screen dates from the early nineteenth century (it is reputedly by Cockerell) and includes a fine central arch surmounted by statues of a horse and two eagles. In contrast to the severe exterior of the house, the interior is surprisingly elegant. A carved oak staircase leads from the spacious entrance hall to the Long Gallery, and the well-proportioned Salon, beautifully decorated with excellent plasterwork. A portrait of Richard Wagner commemorates a visit of the famous German composer to Nanteos. The purpose of Wagner's visit is obscure, but during his stay he must have seen the famous Nanteos Cup, or *Cwpan* as this relic of the Holy Grail is otherwise known. There is, therefore, no reason to doubt the tradition that part of Wagner's opera *Parsifal,* which is based on the story of the Grail, was indeed composed here. The *Cwpan* can still be seen at Nanteos although it is now little more than a couple of fragments of blackened wood riveted together. Reputedly, it was the cup brought by Joseph of Arimathea to the Celtic monastery of Glastonbury. After that it was brought to Ystrad Fflur for safe keeping and finally, after the dissolution of the abbey, to Nanteos.

Overlooking Aberystwyth's natural harbour where the Ystwyth and Rheidol join together, is Pen Dinas, a whaleback hill rising steeply out of the sea. A nineteenth-century column in the shape of a cannon (in honour of the Duke of Wellington and the Battle of Waterloo) dominates the top of the 400-foot hill. Today, there is nothing except sheep, but two thousand and more years ago this was the site of an immense Iron-Age fort. Actually, there are two separate forts which were later joined together by great multiple ramparts, still plainly visible, to create a single hour-glass-shaped redoubt. Obviously this must have been a very important fort, for it commanded the routes of the two most important valleys inland, and at the same time guarded the coastal route between north and south.

Pen Dinas is an excellent vantage point from which to look down on Aberystwyth. From this bird's-eye view one can identify many of the features that form the fabric and history of the town. Immediately, to the north, is the fishing harbour and behind this are the ruins of the bastide castle and parish church with the medieval pattern of the street layout still clear in the rear; on the sea front are the pier, the promenade lined with hotels and the older buildings of the university college; inland on the hill to the right is the National Library and the new university campus, while still further east, on the edge of the Rheidol valley at Llanbadarn Fawr, is the ancient church of Padarn on its Celtic site.

Today Aberystwyth is a flourishing holiday resort, administrative centre and university town all rolled into one. The town has an essentially Victorian and early Edwardian appearance, even though its history as the parish of Llanbadarn goes back to the Middle Ages and even earlier. The sea front is gracefully curved and the entire length of the promenade is backed by four- and five-storey terraces terminated at either end by larger buildings which in turn are flanked by the dominating shapes of Pen Dinas and Constitution Hill.

The University College at the southern end of the promenade is a real eye-catcher, though not surprisingly for this remarkable building started life as an exotic hotel and not as a college. Its beginnings go back to 1864 when the railway was brought to Aberystwyth and Thomas Savin, the contractor for the railway, decided to develop the town as an extra-special tourist resort. Savin bought the old Castle House (originally built for Uvedale Price by John Nash) and called in John Seddon to enlarge it into a grandiose hotel. Seddon's ideas for the building were nothing short of a neo-Gothic fantasy. Savin was impatient to get the hotel completed and work proceeded at a fantastic pace, and often ahead of the architect's drawings, until after spending £80,000 on the hotel in just over a year, Savin went bankrupt. The building was sold at a fraction of this cost in 1872 and Seddon was recalled to adapt it and enlarge it again as the first college of the newly formed University of Wales. Seddon's design this time was even more spectacular than the original and envisaged a rich mixture of Early Gothic and Perpendicular architecture with Tudor half-timbering and romantic pinnacles, castellated towers and turrets. All this was of course quite unsuited to what was basically a non-conformist college, but, nevertheless, had the building been completed as intended, it would have been one of the great monuments of Victoriar architecture in Britain. Instead, the building was gutted by a disastrous fire in 1885, still incomplete. From the ruins only the triangular southern section, the richly decorated northern wing and the boldly conceived circular tower and entrance at the rear survived, all the other parts being later additions.

The streets behind the college are well worth exploring for their pleasant terraces and interesting architecture. In Laura Place there is an elegant Regency building with tall round-headed windows and overhanging roof, that was built in 1820 as the town's

Assembly Rooms and later became a Students' Union. Nearby, in New Street is Aberystwyth's oldest chapel, the diminutive Unitarian Meeting House, its geometrical shapes sharply defined in black-and-white. Capel St Paul (1879) in Great Darkgate Street is, by contrast, majestic in scale, with giant Corinthian columns marking the entrance. Almost opposite, where the clocktower now stands, was once the site of the old Town Hall. Further along the road is a plaque above a shop commemorating (in Welsh, for this is still the language of most of the permanent residents), the formation of the Calvinistic Methodists' Confession of Faith in 1823.

Beyond the grassy churchyard of the St Michael's parish church (1890) lie the storm ravaged ruins of the castle on its superb site overlooking the sea. This was one of Edward I's earliest castles in Wales, and was erected after the unfortunate defeat of Llywelyn II at the hands of the English king in the First War of Independence (1276-77). The foundations of the borough date from this period when Edward I laid out the streets and town walls alongside the castle. In the early fifteenth century the castle became one of the strongholds of the hero, Owain Glyndŵr in the third War of Independence and it was here that he sealed his treaty with Charles IV of France. Two centuries later Thomas Bushell established a mint within the castle. Out of his profits Bushell was able to lend Charles I of England £40,000, raise a regiment of soldiers from his lead miners and clothe the whole Royalist army for the Civil War. This, however, turned out to be a poor investment, for in 1646 the castle was destroyed by the Parliamentarians.

At the northern end of the sea front Constitution Hill raises steeply out of the sea. The upper part of the hill has been laid out in gardens and a funicular railway takes the visitor effortlessly to the top from whence there is a magnificently panoramic view of the whole of Cardigan Bay from the Llŷn peninsula, in the north, to Penmaen Dewi (St David's Head) in the south.

Apart from the allurement of the sea, one of the main attractions of Aberystwyth is the Rheidol narrow-gauge railway, with its steam engines and smart blue carriages. It runs (in summer) 12 miles from Aberystwyth along the side of the Rheidol valley in a sinuous scenic route, in and out of the woods and forests and climbing all the time, to Pontarfynach (Devil's Bridge).

From its narrow peninsula between the Afon Rheidol and the sea, Aberystwyth has grown rapidly eastwards and up the sides of the valley. High above the town centre at Penglais are two of the town's most important institutions. The first of these is the National Library of Wales, built between 1911 and 1937 and financed mostly by the voluntary contributions of ordinary Welsh people. It has a pompous classical white stone front and a nondescript red brick rear. As an architectural monument to a nation devoted to literature and poetry it is sadly disappointing and reflects neither the Wales of the past, nor the artistic ferment of the twentieth century. The interior is better and that, after all, is the important thing about a library. Here is the finest collection of Welsh books and manuscripts, including the oldest manuscript in the Welsh language, the twelfth-century *Llyfr Du Caerfyrddin* (Black Book of Carmarthen), and the manuscripts of the *Mabinogion* and the *Laws of Hywel Dda*. Although the emphasis, naturally, is on Welsh literature and books about Wales, there are many other valuable items in this treasure house, such as a valuable manuscript of Chaucer's *Canterbury Tales*, and a superb collection of early French romances. There is also an exhibition gallery open during the summer months.

Behind and above the National Library are the newer buildings of the University College. At present the development of this campus is only partly complete and forms a rather heterogeneous collection. The climax of the scheme is the imposing Great Hall in the centre of the site. Flanked on either side by the College Library and the Students' Union, it faces on to a high-level open court containing a tall, angular bell-tower. Before entering the Great Hall it is worth stopping and turning around to look out across the court to take in the superb view of the town and Cardigan Bay spread out like a vast map below – on a sunny day the pinnacled walls and towers of the old college, the parish church and the castle stand out in golden buff silhouetted against an azure sea background. Inside the Great Hall stairs lead up the main concourse, and then up again to an exhibition gallery and on to the

Theatr y Werin (a comfortable and pleasantly decorated auditorium) at the rear of the complex.

Llanbadarn Fawr lies alongside the Afon Rheidol below the university campus and inland from Aberystwyth. It is now a suburb of the larger town, but its history goes back much farther. The massive parish church overshadowing the village was built in the early thirteenth century on the site of a monastery founded by St Padarn in the sixth century. Cruciform in plan with no aisles it has few decorative features inside – just plain white walls and a few narrow lancet windows placed high up on the nave walls. This extreme simplicity, however, gives it an austere dignity in keeping with its early origins. A reminder of the early days when Llanbadarn was one of the chief monastic centres in Wales, are the two Celtic crosses in the south transept. One of these, probably dating from the tenth century, is richly ornamented with complex interwoven patterning. There is a memorial slab set in the chancel floor to Lewis Morris (1706-65), a distinguished Anglesey poet who lived the last years of his life at Penbryn near Llanbadarn Fawr. He came to Ceredigion as sub-steward of the Crown Lands but failed to get on with the local squires who had lead mining rights from the Crown. He was bitterly persecuted and even thrown into prison on one occasion, but in spite of these setbacks he was able to devote much of his time to writing humorous verse and collecting ancient poetry.

The greatest of Welsh medieval poets, Dafydd ap Gwilym has no memorial here, although he is reputed to have been born nearby at Penryhn-coch and went to services at Llanbadarn church. As we known from his own poems, however, he was usually more interested in the girls in the congregation than in the service and perhaps, therefore, the vicar was not too keen to immortalise the poet.

There is a halt on the Rheidol narrow gauge railway at Llanbadarn Fawr and one can travel up the valley to Devil's Bridge by that rare means of locomotion the stream train, or alternatively and more comfortably, but less romantically, by car on the road via Capel Bangor and Aber-ffrwd. At Capel Bangor the main road leaves the Rheidol to follow the Melindwr past Goginan and its abandoned lead workings and up into the hills at Ponterwyd, but a secondary road descends to the Rheidol itself at Aber-ffrwd. Here is the first of three reservoirs that together form the Rheidol Hydro-Electric Scheme. The lowest reservoir, the Cwm Rheidol, is a regulating reservoir built to ensure that the amount of water flowing in the Afon Rheidol does not fall below a certain limit. Great pains have been taken in the design of the reservoir and its associated works to ensure that they fit into the surrounding landscape with as little intrusive effect as possible. At the foot of the reservoir, for instance (where one would normally expect to see an alien-looking dam across the gorge) the original waterfall has been cut back 90 feet upstream to form a rocky weir and a landscaped viewing terrace has been constructed alongside. The main power station (open to visitors) is further upstream at the side of the man-made lake and has been designed as an innocuous square block, faced in local stone. A three-mile-long tunnel has been bored through the mountain and this carries the water under pressure from the middle reservoir down to the power station to drive turbines and generate electricity.

The narrow-gauge railway, cut into the side of the valley, climbs up and up and eventually reaches Devil's Bridge, or Pontarfynach, some 100 yards above the turbulent Afon Rheidol. Here, where the Rheidol changes course abruptly to follow the original valley of the Teifi, the Afon Mynach cascades down into the gorge to join the main river. Afon Mynach means Monk's river and Pontarfynach, the correct name of Devil's Bridge, refers to the earliest and lowest of the three bridges across the stream. This was built in 1087 (and still stands after nearly 900 years) by the monks of Ystrad Fflur who held large sheep-farming estates in the area. In 1708 another bridge was built immediately above the first and this was eventually followed by the modern iron bridge that now carries the main road. The earliest bridge is also known in Welsh as Pont-y-gwr-drwg, or 'Bridge of the Evil One'. According to legend this was built by the Devil as part of a bargain with Marged, an old country woman. The Devil appeared to Marged in the disguise of a monk and offered to build the bridge for her on condition that he should possess the first living creature to cross it. The wily old woman foiled Satan's plan, however, by throwing a bone across the new bridge, thus enticing her hungry dog to dash across it first, whereupon the 'monk' struck the ground three times with his hoof and vanished in a cloud of smoke.

At the side of the triple bridge stands the Hafod Arms Hotel, an unexpected structure looking like an overgrown Swiss chalet but eminently at home in its sub-Alpine surroundings. It dates from the 1820's and was built by the Duke of Newcastle when he bought the Hafod Uchtryd estate. In 1854 the indefatigable George Borrow slept there and described it as 'an immense lofty cottage with projecting eaves, and has a fine window to the east which enlightens a stately staircase and a noble gallery'.

From the wide terrace opposite the hotel one can look down into the forest-filled Rheidol gorge, but to see the waterfalls in all their dramatic beauty it is necessary to go back down the road and pay at the turnstile on the far side of the bridge. A footpath from the turnstile climbs steeply down 102 steps, known to tourists as 'Jacob's Ladder', to a bridge below the magnificent series of seething cataracts, of which the largest has a drop of 112 feet, known collectively as the Mynach Falls. There are strategically placed viewing platforms on the way down and once across the Mynach stream the footpath winds up on the far side back to the top again. Other footpaths lead to the almost equally fine Nant Lletty Falls nearby and to a vantage point overlooking a splendid view of the Cyfarllwyd Falls on the Rheidol.

The Cyfarllwyd Falls themselves stand at the lower end of a narrow twisting chasm through which the Rheidol dashes on its impetuous journey to the sea. At the upper end of the chasm amidst the most romantic scenery an iron bridge – said to have been built by the local vicar and hence its name Parson's Bridge – crosses the river. A steep path leads up from the bridge to Ysbyty Cynfyn church. The ancient churchyard, or *llan*, of the church is particularly interesting for not only is it circular, denoting an Early Christian foundation, but it incorporates the remains of a Bronze-Age stone circle. Thus this spot has probably been in use as a religious site for well over 3,000 years. Such an astonishing continuity of use is not uncommon for Welsh church sites, but is almost unknown elsewhere in western Europe. Of the original monoliths forming the stone circle only five remain, one of which is more than ten feet high.

The Afon Rheidol rises in a small lake known as Llygad Rheidol ('Eye of Rheidol') at the foot of the main peak of Pumlumon which at 2,468 feet is the highest point in mid-Wales. No one knows for sure the derivation of the name Pumlumon, but the commonly accepted meaning is 'five peaks'. The easiest approach to the mountain is from the south at Eisteddfa Gurig. The path follows the tumbling course of a stream for a long way and passes an old leadmine, but it is not really a very interesting way – the easy routes very rarely are – for from this angle Pumlumon looks nothing more than barren moorland. A far more attractive route is to take the mountain road from Ponterwyd and follow the Rheidol to its source. On the way the road passes the ruined cottage of Aber Ceiro Fach, birthplace of Sir John Rhys (1840-1915) the first professor of Celtic at Oxford University, and the Nant-y-Moch Reservoir. From Llyn Llygad Rheidol there is a steep and exhausting scramble up the craggy north side to the summit.

Though from a distance Pumlumon appears gentle enough it is in reality a wild place with many boggy areas and on days when bad weather comes down suddenly it can be dangerous to the incautious. However, on fine days the effort to get to the top is more than compensated for by the wonderful panorama that unfolds. The view covers most of Wales as well as Cardigan Bay, for this is the centre point of the country. On a very clear day one can see to the north the peaks of Cadair Idris and Yr Wyddfa (Snowdon) the island of Enlli (Bardsey) and the Llŷn peninsula; south-west the prospect extends down the broad Teifi valley to Mynydd Preseli and the Pembroke peninsula; southwards are the vast expanses of the Elenydd moorlands and beyond the shapely peaks of the Brecon Beacons and Black Mountains; and to the east is the ancient principality of Powys, the Border Marchlands and England. Closer at hand look down and see the five rivers from which perhaps Pumlumon also takes its name – the Dulas and Clywedog to the north-east, the Rheidol on the north-western side, the Wye (Gwy in Welsh) immediately to the south-east and to the east the source of the longest river in Britain, the Severn or Hafren.

Numerous lakes lie dotted around the foothills of Pumlumon. By far the largest sheet of water, however, is the man-made lake of Nant-y-Moch, its twin arms curling around the base of the oddly terraced Drosgol mountain as though embracing it. The dam for this, the main reservoir in the Rheidol Hydro-Electric Scheme, has been built to a colossal scale in keeping with its surroundings. In a different colour or material the gigantic sloping buttresses and arches would be magnificently impressive; but the raw colour of the concrete can look harshly white on a bright sunny day and the dam then imposes itself unsympathetically on the landscape.

The mountain road from Ponterwyd to Tal-y-bont crosses the dam, opening up what was until recently a treeless wilderness. It was not always an uninhabited wilderness, however, for a hundred years ago numerous leadmines were working and the now ruined farms and cottages were all occupied. Now trees are being planted but though there are plenty of visitors few people live in the area. Birds are scarce too, probably because of the absence of deciduous trees, but if one is lucky one can see the rare fork-tailed red kite gliding and diving and skidding along with the air currents at the northernmost limit of its range.

A narrow but well-paved mountain road follows the west bank of the reservoir, from where there is a good view of Pumlumon, and then follows the delightful Camdwr valley. At the end of the valley the road turns sharply west and drops down suddenly through the appropriately named Bwlch-y-garreg (Pass of the Rock) to emerge within view of the sea in the broad and deeply trenched valley of Cwm Ceulan.

Tal-y-bont is a pleasantly compact village and quite large for these parts. The main attraction of the place is the stone woollen mill beside the river. Its century-old waterwheel still works and the original hand-loom weaving machinery (dating from the establishment of the mill in 1809) is still used for making tweeds.

North of Tal-y-bont is Tre Taliesin, the fictional birthpace of Taliesin, the sixth-century Celtic bard. One folk legend in the *Mabinogion* tells of the birth of Taliesin after various transformations from a blue salmon to a dog, from a dog to a stag and so on until he became a grain of wheat and was swallowed by the goddess Ceridwen who had taken on the form of a black hen; 'for nine nights I was in her crop. I have been dead, I have been alive, I am Taliesin'.

A prehistoric burial chamber above the village, known as Bedd Taliesin and comprising a large flat slab resting on four smaller stones, is the mythological grave of the bard. Taliesin, however, is no myth but was the *pencerdd* or chief poet of Urien, a north British prince who reigned at the end of the sixth century. The poet himself wrote 'my original country is the region of the summer stars ... hereafter all kings shall call me Taliesin'. Though Taliesin was almost certainly never anywhere near what today is known as Wales, the language in which he wrote his poetry was the forerunner of modern Welsh. Appropriately, some of his poems, composed eight centuries before the time of Chaucer, are now preserved in *Llyfr Taliesin* (the book of Taliesin) at the National Library in Aberyswyth.

In prehistoric times, or perhaps even more recently, Tre Taliesin was at the edge of the Dyfi estuary. Now a vast peat bog known as Cors Fochno separates the village from the estuary and the sea. Like Cors Goch Glanteifi at Tregaron, it is rich in wild life and is now a national nature reserve. From the main road it appears as an impenetrable brown marshland with slight hills standing out here and there like islands, as indeed they were at one time. In fact most of the farms in this area have *ynys,* meaning island, incorporated in their names. But as one travels towards the sea there are flat green moors through which a straight channel has been cut to divert the Afon Leri. The original course of the Leri, now a land-locked serpentine lake, is further west a few yards behind the sand dunes that separate it from the sea. Further north the sand dunes become miniature mountains and have formed a promontory jutting out into the estuary from what was less than a century ago an island called Twyni Bach. From the tip of Twyni Bach the small town of Aberdyfi, nestling below the hills of Meirion on the other side of the water, seems to be a mere stone's throw away.

A superb sandy beach stretches down the coast for four miles as far as Borth and then peters out against the rocky cliffs. Borth itself

is an unexciting and elongated town of a thousand people but only
one street. Its architecure is a peculiar mixture of styles, so that
even the old rustic stone cottages seem out of place here. What
Borth lacks of contemporary interest is made up for by folklore
which ascribes to this part of the coast the story of Cantre'r
Gwaelod, the Lowland Hundred. The legendary Cantre'r Gwaelod
was supposed to have been a large tract of low-lying land belonging
to Prince Gwyddno which, according to the thirteenth-century
Black Book of Carmarthen, was overwhelmed by the water which a
maiden had let loose from the well after feasting too much. With
the passage of time the tale became modified and improved;
Cantre'r Gwaelod became the whole of Cardigan Bay from the
Llŷn peninsula to the mouth of the Afon Teifi and the well became
a great embankment the sluices of which were left open by a
drunkard named Seithennin in the sixth century.

Writers have claimed that Sarn Gynfelyn, a stony bank near
Borth which extends into Cardigan Bay for a considerable distance,
and Sarn Badrid off the coast of Meirionydd are the remains of the
dams built to keep out the sea. They are, however, entirely natural
ridges of loose rocks. Nevertheless the coast of Cardigan Bay show
unmistakable signs of having subsided since prehistoric times.
Solidified tree stumps can still be seen, for instance, on the sands
north of Borth between high and low tides and these mark the
position of what was once an extensive forest. Perhaps, when all the
later elaborations have been stripped off the story, the legend of
Cantre'r Gwaelod does after all represent a distant memory of a
period in prehistoric times when the level of the sea was much lower
than it is at present. We shall never know the truth, but it is nice to
think that the legend has some factual basis, for continuity with the
past is one of the distinguishing traits of Wales and of Ceredigion in
particular.

Index

NOTE The spelling of place names is nearly always a minor stumbling block in writing about Wales. For the majority of villages and small towns there is no difficulty as these are usually orthographically correct in their spelling. Where a place is commonly known by an English name, such as Newport or Fishguard, there is similarly no difficulty. The problem of spelling arises in the relatively small number of towns where a Welsh name has, over the years, become partly anglicised; Often the anglicisation is of a very minor nature and reversion to the original form is unlikely to cause confusion. As a general rule, where there is only a difference of one or two letters between the commonly accepted but incorrect English version and the correct Welsh version then the Welsh form has been used. For example Llandaf is used instead of Llandaff.